REMEMBER

Eternity

The Journey Continues

J. E. STARKS-BROWN

authorHOUSE®

AuthorHouse™
1663 Liberty Drive
Bloomington, IN 47403
www.authorhouse.com
Phone: 1 (800) 839-8640

This is a work of fiction. All of the characters, names, incidents,
organizations, and dialogue in this novel are either the products
of the author's imagination or are used fictitiously.

Published by AuthorHouse 10/14/2017

ISBN: 978-1-5462-0363-6 (sc)
ISBN: 978-1-5462-0362-9 (e)

Print information available on the last page.

Any people depicted in stock imagery provided by Thinkstock are models,
and such images are being used for illustrative purposes only.
Certain stock imagery © Thinkstock.

This book is printed on acid-free paper.

Because of the dynamic nature of the Internet, any web addresses or links contained in
this book may have changed since publication and may no longer be valid. The views
expressed in this work are solely those of the author and do not necessarily reflect the
views of the publisher, and the publisher hereby disclaims any responsibility for them.

Scripture quotations marked KJV are from the Holy Bible, King James Version
(Authorized Version). First published in 1611. Quoted from the KJV Classic
Reference Bible, Copyright © 1983 by The Zondervan Corporation.

Acknowledgement

To my brother Norman who faithfully took the time to read and encouraged me to continue in that which was given to me by the Author and Finisher of our faith. For this, I simply say Thank-you.

INTRODUCTION

"Remember Eternity", as its title suggests, is a reminder to us all that there is life beyond this present in which we now live. It is a fictional look into the lives of a group of not so ordinary Spirit filled people in the process of making preparations for Eternity. Set in the city of present day Des Moines, Iowa, the intention of "Remember Eternity is to help the reader get beyond what we see with our natural or carnal minds and to become focused on the spiritual and that which is eternal.

The story line revolves around the day to day challenges in the family of Frances Michaels, her son Paul and three daughters, Irene, Christine and Donna; their spouses Jane, Douglas, James and Randy, respectively. As the mother of four and grandmother of forty-one, Frances is recognized as a matriarchal symbol of God given wisdom coupled with abundant experiences. She is ever nurturing, advising, and whether solicited or no, her words are lovingly accepted with grace.

Paul, the stern and serious high school principal, Douglas the prosperous insurance executive, James the successful architech and Randy the public transit operator all come together to create a scenario of events and situations. As Paul, Christine and their spouses face the challenges of their interracial marriages, they ultimately become stronger in their faith in God. He becomes their battle axe and strength in adversity when other extended family members come into play. Sensitive issues arise but are successfully overcome by proven spiritual weapons of warfare which is the basic foundation and theme of "Remember Eternity." It is intended to reinforce spiritual perspectives in an increasingly Anti-Christ society and although unpopular and often tedious, doing it God's way ultimately insures victory.

As the journey continues, Michael is found rejoicing on the day of his spiritual birthday after "coming out of the wilderness" of the world. He soon gets his first opportunity to be a witness to younger sister Terry, caught up in the snare of prostitution and promiscuity which eventually leads her to a near death experience. As he and older brother Douglas continue to hold her up in constant intercessory prayer, grace and mercy prevail as" God is not willing that any should perish."

Follow the emotional and sensitive matters that emerge as this family discovers that "Many are the afflictions of the righteous but the Lord delivereth him out of them all." (Psalms 34:19) KJV. As Michael and Janice begin a courtship, they endure ridicule and soul searching issues while acknowledging God for direction.

Finally, "Remember Eternity" is an intimate look into a family's struggles, victories, trials and tribulations which are all a part of the sanctified set apart life that God is calling for in these troubling and stressful times.

FOREWORD

In these perilous and uncertain times, there remains one undeniable fact that we all must face and that is Eternity. As we live our everyday lives, year in and year out, we are ever moving closer to the era where time will be an extinct entity. In our human natures, we tend to view Eternity as a fact that is eons away or something to be dealt with after we tend to our own temporal agendas.

The Word of God leaves no doubt about the two eternal destinations that we have the options to choose from. Eternal reward in Heaven or eternal damnation in Hell leaves no choice to the reasonable mind and this being said, it only makes sense to "Remember Eternity".

In this society, we are bombarded with countless winds of doctrine that have forms of godliness while denying the power thereof which is a danger to the eternal soul. Ephesians 4:5 (KJV) plainly states that there is One Lord, one faith, one baptism. This one Lord, Jesus Christ, commanded us in St. Matthew 28:19 to be baptized in the name of the Father (Jesus), the name of the Son (Jesus) and the name of the Holy Ghost (Jesus), not His titles. This was confirmed through the Apostle Peter on the Day of Pentecost (Acts 2:38), when three thousand souls were added on the Birth Day of the Church. The ingredients of genuine godly sorrow or repentance from sin, water baptism in the name of Jesus for the remission or removal of sin, coupled with the baptism of the Holy Ghost. The undeniable evidence of this second birth experience is the speaking in other tongues as the Spirit of God gives the utterance. There is no substitute for this awesome encounter with God that empowers the born again believer to overcome the sinful Adamic nature that we are all enter into this world with. It is not to be scoffed at or minimized by those who would downplay its significance or importance.

"Remember Eternity" is an intimate look into a family's struggles, victories, trials and tribulations of the righteous which are all a part of the sanctified set apart life that God is calling for in these troubling and stressful times.

CHAPTER 1

APRIL 19, SUNDAY

"You know that she's my new best friend now don't you?" Michael asked Sunday night at the kitchen table with Douglas and Irene after church.

"You can't have her, I had her first." Douglas told him, referring to Frances.

"Didn't I tell you the other day that she could probably help you out?" Irene asked him.

"You did but I had no idea just how much." He said shaking his head. "I mean that woman is dynamite and I really don't think I'd be sittin' here with the Holy Ghost now if she hadn't done what she did."

"Okay Michael back up, how did you end up over there in the first place?" She asked him. "I wanna know the whole story because when Sheila came and told me that all of that noise and commotion was about you, I was in shock." She said. "I was up in the nursery so I couldn't really see what was goin' on 'til I saw them helpin' you up to the pool and that's when I lost it."

"I don't even remember too much about that but when I woke up this mornin', you had already left and I decided to go over there and thank her for prayin' over me the other day, because I really don't think that I would have this job if she hadn't done that."

"You might be right."

"I think I am but anyway, I was tellin' her how I couldn't stop thinkin' about what I felt by the time she got through with me that day."

"What day was this?" Irene asked him.

"This was the day that your father came home, Wednesday I think it was." He said, after thinking a moment. "She had me cryin' like a baby and I don't do that but she told me that I wasn't able to forget about that because that's what my soul was cravin' and it wasn't gonna let me alone 'til it was satisfied." He barely got out as he became overwhelmed in his spirit at what had happened to him. "Oh my God, I feel like I'm in a dream, this can't be me."

"But it is you honey and you don't know how happy and excited we are for you." Irene told him.

"I'm happy and excited for me too 'cause you just don't know what I have been through in my mind for the last month."

"But God knew and He worked things out because that's what He does." Douglas told him. "And He knows how to get you to the place where He can help you and that's what happened to you this mornin.'"

"Man did it ever." He said. "But then she asked me if I had been to church since I've been here and I had to tell her that I hadn't." "So she took over and said that we could go together and that way she wouldn't have to wait on Paul to pick her up." "Then she said that the Lord was gonna meet us there and I'm thinkin' what does she mean by that?" He said, thinking back. "But I know now don't I?" He added, laughing at the thought of his experience with God.

"No doubt about it." Irene said. "But she didn't leave you any choice huh?"

"She didn't, she made that call whether I wanted to or not so when we got there and started to get close to the sanctuary, is that what you call it?"

"That's what you call it." Douglas said.

"It was like the closer we got to it, the more I started feelin' like I did that day with her and that's when I just gave it up." "I took a couple of steps in there and it was over, I felt like I got hit with a lightnin' bolt, I'm not kiddin.'" "And when I was talkin' to James yesterday out at the lot, he told me that if and when this would happen to me, I wouldn't be able to describe it and man he was right on about that."

"So now you know what we're talkin' about." Irene told him. And this is pretty much a whole new beginnin' for you so take advantage of it and don't be afraid to ask for help when you have questions because you will, believe me."

"After what just happened to me it feels like I can handle anything that goes down but that's good to know." He said. "And that reminds me, Terry called me yesterday and she told me some stuff that you're not gonna like." He told Douglas, referring to their youngest sister.

"Did she call just to talk or was it for somethin' else?" Douglas asked him after a moment.

"I hadn't talked to her since I left so I think she just wanted to see how things were goin' up here but she told me that she's been doin' the streets down there for extra money." "And lovin' it she said."

"Is that so?" Douglas asked him after a moment. "The last time I talked to her, she was thinkin' about goin' to school, what happened with that?"

"She didn't say anything about that but she did say somethin' about comin' up here to visit for a couple of days since I'm not goin' back down there."

"She probably misses you." Irene said.

"She said she did and I might be able to go down there after tomorrow's job orientation."

"Did she say how long she's been doin' that?" Douglas asked him, becoming obviously concerned.

"She said her hours got cut at the store where she works and she had to do somethin' to make up for it and that was the first thing she thought about doin.'"

"Does she know how dangerous that is?' Douglas asked, disturbed.

"I really don't think she's worried about that, she said she knows how to take care of herself."

"How old is she, twenty?" Irene asked.

"She'll be twenty next month." Douglas said. "But I'm glad that I know about that little conversation because this isn't somethin' that we can just let go and say that's her problem." He continued. "I might just have to go down there and help her out, you know what I mean?"

"I knew that you would be on that and if you need me to go with you, let me know." Michael said. "And I need to talk to you about somethin' else too so when you get a minute."

"What's wrong with now?"

"I hear one of the kids callin' me; perfect timing." Irene said as she got up from the table.

"I just had a question about your daughter and since I don't quite know her well enough to talk to her about it, I figured that you would know." He began.

"She won't bite you, she's harmless believe me."

"Are you sure that her baby's father isn't around anywhere?" He asked him then.

"He's not, once he found out that she was pregnant, he dropped her and told her that it wasn't his problem."

"Like a thousand other guys do huh?"

"It happens all of the time which is why all five of your nieces are gonna know the facts of life as soon as they're able to make a baby if you get my meanin.'" "I don't care if they're ten years old, it happens and I told Irene the same thing."

"Ten years old Douglas?"

"I processed a claim five or six years ago for a girl that was eleven and a half that had a full term baby so it's not impossible and nowdays when anything goes, we can't be too careful." Douglas told him. "And this experience that I've had with Janice has made me more determined to make sure that my other girls won't have to go through what she's had to." "But if they do, it won't be because they weren't taught right from wrong."

"When did she get the Holy Ghost?"

"Just about a month ago so she's just startin' out like you are but she's learnin' really quick about what holiness is about, and the difference in her now and the way she was when she first moved here is like day and night."

"Man I can already tell that somethin' is goin' on with me and it's been what, just twelve hours?" He said as he glanced at his watch.

"And that's what the Holy Ghost does, it's your power to overcome the nature that you're born with and once you learn how to let the Lord help you, livin' right is not hard to do."

"Yeah I was just drivin' around after I had dinner with James and Chris, I was tryin' to wrap my head around what happened and somebody cut me off and I almost had an accident." He said. "And it was like some kind of feelin' of calm or peace whatever you wanna call it took over me and I couldn't believe it." "This time yesterday, I would've cussed and flipped'em off and anything else you can think of but all of that just wasn't there." "It was unreal."

"But that was the Lord showin' you exactly what you have now and I don't care what kind of problems you might have, nothin' is worth givin' up your salvation." Douglas told him. "You'll have some times where you might feel like throwin' your hands up over situations and you might not understand why you're goin' through certain things but whatever you do, make sure that you have a relationship with the Lord by stayin' on your knees, that's where your victories come from."

"Is that how you're able to handle everything like it's nothin'?" Michael asked him. "I've been watchin' how you don't let anything trip you out and it was like, how is he handlin' all of this stuff that's goin' down without losin' it, you know what I mean?"

"It's because I've learned how to give things up that I know are too big for me to do anything about and nothin' is too big or too small for God to do." He answered after a moment. "Like this thing that you just laid on me about Terry, that's a case for the Lord and that's somethin' that both of us need to start takin' to the throne and I mean a.s.a.p."

"I couldn't believe how matter-of-fact she was about it and I know that I don't have a spotless reputation, you know that, but to say that you can't wait to hit the streets and that's all she thinks about, that's a problem."

"How did that come up anyway?"

"She wanted to know if I had found a job yet and when I told her what was goin' on, she told me that she was makin' money the easy way." He said. "And that's when she tried to go into all of this detail about what she was doin' but that's when I had to shut her down, she didn't need to go there with me, as much as I've seen and done." "It was TMI big time."

"That sounds like she's wantin' out but doesn't know how to ask for the help." Douglas said. "And like I said before, I might just have to make a trip down there so stand by, two is better than one."

"So if she calls me back, I don't have any problem tellin' her that you know about what she's doin'."

"That's up to you but I have enough sense to know that I don't have the power to go down there and force her into doin' anything that she doesn't want to do."

"But you have to try because if somethin' would happen, it would be a hard thing to get over Douglas." "Why don't you call her first?" He suggested.

"She doesn't have her own place does she?"

"Not yet, that's what she's tryin' to do but since her hours got cut, it's makin' it harder for her so workin' the streets is the easy way to make some quick money accordin' to her."

"I'll get back with you about this, thanks for the info." He told him after a moment. "And the Lord is startin' to use you already so get your mind ready."…

APRIL 21, TUESDAY

"So your orientation was yesterday and you start workin' the over night shift beginnin' Monday night?" Sheila asked as she, Michael and 'Nita sat at the table at Chris and James' after the graveside service for William.

"It's a God thing as you like to say." He said. "So I'll have to get used to bein' up all night but I'll have most of the day free to get other stuff done."

"Are you still gonna be workin' with James out at the lot?" 'Nita asked him.

"Absolutely positively, we got a good start on it last week so we can't stop now."

"Michael Johnson, are you gonna tell me how your mother and father managed to make two babies that look just alike and they're fifteen years apart?" 'Nita asked him then.

"You noticed that huh?"

"How can you not notice it, if you had a beard, you could pass for twins, what's up with that?" She asked him as she scooped out more macaroni and cheese from a serving bowl. "And how did you manage to come all the way up here from St. Louis and get the Holy Ghost before I did?"

"You almost made me choke." Michael told her, laughing at her last question.

"You're gonna have to get used to me, I'm crazy 'Nita Scott and I say whatever is on my mind."

"I see."

"I'm still waitin' on your answer brother man." "How did you do that?"

"I didn't do it, the Lord did it and He'll do it for you too."

"I have issues as you can see, I need to seriously get it together before the Lord comes and I miss the rapture."

'Nita you need to stop, and you remind me so much of the way I used to act and talk before I got some sense." Sheila said.

"It's in the genes, we can't help it."

"When I think about all of that crazy stuff that me and Ruth did when we were livin' here, I almost get sick."

"Like what Sheila, tell me about it."

"Like the time that we just took off one day with the kids and drove to St. Louis to go up in the Gateway Arch without tellin' Chris we were goin.'" "And this was before everybody had a cell phone so we couldn't even call her 'til we got there."

"He told me about that and he said you were givin' her a break from the kids one day but he ended up apologizin' for makin' her worry." Michael said, laughing with her.

"How many times have you been up in there Michael and don't say never because I wouldn't believe it." 'Nita told him.

"Never." He said. "Passed by it all of the time but never made it in there."

"I oughta make you take me and the kids down there on a field trip when school is out." "How long does it take, a couple of hours?"

"You would have to be doin' some heavy duty speedin' to get there in two hours, it's more like three and a half if you do seventy all the way there." He said as he noticed Janice come in the kitchen.

"They're goin' out to the lot if anybody wants to go." She said as she sat plates on the counter.

"Who is they?" 'Nita asked. "I haven't been yet and since I'm gonna be livin' out there, I probably need to go and check it out."

James and Chris and Paul and Jane are goin', and I'm stayin' here with the kids." "They're takin' some and leavin' some."

"I'll stay here and help you with 'em." Michael told her. "I was just out there yesterday so I know what's goin' on." He added as he got up to empty an overflowing trash bag.

"I know that he was my father and all of that but I couldn't make myself really feel anything." Janice remarked half an hour later on the front porch with Michael. "Is that wrong?" She asked him as she opened a jar of baby food for Byron.

"I wouldn't call it wrong because you didn't know him like that." "You have his biology and that's it but anybody can do that."

"And if I had known that Marie and me are just half sisters I wouldn't have taken that as hard as I did but I can't keep thinkin' about it because it'll make me feel worse."

"Have you talked to your mother yet?"

She shook her head. "But I really should do that because I can't forget what Douglas told me about not holdin' anything against her and the quicker I do it, the better it'll be I guess."

"Has he ever talked to you about havin' a relationship with the Lord?" He asked her then. "We were talkin' Sunday night about all of this and I didn't know that that was even possible, because up 'til now I just thought of God as bein' somethin' way out there out of reach."

"I did too 'til this happened and I remember him tellin' me to find some time everyday to talk to the Lord and it makes so much difference when you do." Janice said as she wiped baby food from Byron's hands. "And Irene told me that's the reason why it's so easy for him to help and talk to people."

"So in other words, because he's always prayin' it's easy for him to make a lot of difference to people."

"And I'll be glad when I can do that because if I'm able to help somebody else by talkin' about how I got over, it's all worth it."

"I can't get over how mature you sound, you must've really gone through some stuff to make you talk like you do."

"I had to grow up quick when I found out that I was pregnant and had to leave D.C. but there's still somethin' in me that needs to know that I have somebody that I can really trust, you know what I mean?"

"James and Douglas huh?"

"My brother and my father." She said with pride and confidence. "And I know that everybody is probably tired of hearin' me say that but those things mean a lot when you've had such bad experiences with other people that you thought you could trust."

"I don't get tired of hearin' that because it's good to know that there are still people around like that and everybody's not a thug."

"They're not and if I have a girl, I'm makin' sure that she has somebody that she can depend on so she won't have to go through some of the things that I had to."

"So you don't know what you're having?"

"I'm havin' my sonogram on Friday." She said after a moment. "And Chris is goin' with me because I have no idea what all of that's about but I'm about to find out."

"It's good that you have such a strong support system around here and I don't ever hear anybody complainin' about havin' to go out of the way to do things for somebody else and it's just so different from what I'm used to." Michael commented.

"And that's why I wasn't gonna let my mother talk me into goin' back to D.C. with her." Janice said. "I'm learnin' how to love people and how to get out of myself and it wasn't anything but a lot of trouble and mess goin' on all of the time and God knew just how to get me away from all of that."

"No regrets huh?" He asked her as he fumbled with his keys.

"None but this time last year if somebody had told me that I would be here livin' like this, I would've told you that you were crazy." 'And you too probably."

"And you know it, this time last month even." "It was just about six weeks ago that I got laid off and I called Douglas two weeks ago to see if anything might be worth comin' up here for and the rest is history as they say." He added. "But I want to be really honest with you about a couple of things so I think that you need to know that I'm interested in more than a friendship with you."

"Michael are you serious?" She asked after a stunned moment.

"I'm serious, I won't be lyin' to you about anything and I think that you know why now and I wouldn't say that if I didn't mean it."

"I'm havin' somebody else's baby Michael, how could you be interested?" She asked him, still in mild shock.

"I think I know that young lady and I've already let your father know that I was gonna have this conversation with you so he would know what might be goin' on."

"Was he as surprised as I am?" Janice asked him as she sat back in her chair.

"I don't think that he was but he made sure I knew that if we decide to go with it, that we need to take it as slow as molasses in January." He said laughing. "He told me that he doesn't want you stressin' out over relationship stuff because you have enough on your plate as it is and he's right about that, I already know."

She nodded a little as she "heard him out."

"Then he made sure that I knew how important it is that both of us get a really good foothold as far as our salvation goes and that is so awesome to me." Michael said as he thought back to their conversation the night before. "He even said somethin' like you can fall as hard as you want, just don't neglect your salvation."

"Wow Michael, I'm just a little bit in shock right now." She said. "You have to understand that I had just made up in my mind that nobody would want to be mixed up with me because of this baby and I'm trippin.'" She admitted.

"I don't really understand that myself but it is what it is Janice." He told her. "Maybe this is a God thing as Sheila says all of the time but for some reason, that doesn't matter to me." "And this was why I asked Douglas if he was really sure that the father wasn't involved anymore because that could get sticky, you know what I mean?"

"I know it could but I'm not even gonna bother him about support or anything because I found out really quick that I was just somebody that he used up for what he wanted." She said. "And I was stupid enough to fall for that but you live and learn as Aunt Frances says."

"My best friend." He said laughing again. "Me and Douglas are fightin' over her, he said that he had her first."

She nodded again as she attempted to absorb what he had said to her.

"Just think about it, and I don't want you to feel any pressure about this but I'm serious." He added as his ringtone sounded. "Hey Terry." He said a moment later as he stood up and walked back into the house.

"What're you doin'?" She asked him.

"Not much, what's goin' on?" He asked her cautiously.

"Douglas isn't there with you is he?"

"He's not but I did tell him what was goin' on with you and he's a little bit worried."

"I got busted last night and I'm still here tryin' to get out." She said after a long moment.

"Did you call home?"

"They're out of town, they went on a two week cruise to the Bahamas." She said irritably. "Can you help me get out of here?" "This is my first time here so all I need is five hundred dollars."

"You don't have any of that yourself?"

"Michael I'm makin' a couple of hundred dollars a night and all that's been goin' on my bills so I don't have it."

"I'm gonna have to get hold of Douglas and I'll call you back Terry."

"Do what you have to do, just get me out of here."

"I'm not takin' the time to drive down there, a lot can happen in four hours." Douglas told Michael as he got on his laptop to buy a plane ticket around five-thirty.

"If you need me to go with you let me know, I don't have anything but time right now."

"The next flight to St. Louis leaves here at seven twenty so if you feel like you need to go, we can leave here in an hour and we'll be there by eight forty- five tonight." He said, reading the screen. "Call or text her and let her know we're on the way."

"I could tell that she was really shocked and not expectin' me to go there with her." Michael remarked later, ten minutes into their flight.

"But whatever you do, if you're not sure about takin' that on, don't lead her on then change your mind about it." "That wouldn't be fair to her and that's not how you treat saints of the most High as your best friend says." Douglas added as he worked on his laptop.

"No doubt and she said she figured that nobody would want to get mixed up with her because of the baby and that would have to be somethin' that's proven, you know what I mean?"

"Because anybody can talk so don't get in the habit of sayin' stuff off the top of your head and not followin' through." "God don't like ugly and I wouldn't assume anything until she lets you know one way or another how she feels about whatever you said to her."

"I didn't tell you that Terry's scared of you did I?" Michael asked, changing the subject.

"She doesn't have any reason to be scared of me, I'm harmless." He said after a moment. "But I do need to let her know about how much fire she's playin' with and this might be a good thing; maybe that trip downtown will make her think twice next time she needs some extra money."

"You didn't tell Irene why you came down here did you?" Terry asked as she sat in an airport restaurant with Michael and Douglas two hours later.

"I told her that we were comin' down here because you needed some help." Douglas told her as a waitress set a cup of coffee in front of him.

"Does she know that I'm comin' back with you?"

"She knows, I wouldn't be doin' this unless she knew about it." He said. "And what's this I hear about you bein' afraid of me?"

"David told me some stuff about you before you moved up there to Des Moines that made me scared of you and I don't know how much of it is true but it's because of him." She said, referring to their oldest brother.

"I'm your brother sweetheart, why would I do anything to hurt you?"

"What did he tell you?" Michael asked her.

"He told me some crap about how you were too good lookin' and too smart for your own good and that you carried a gun all the time." She began.

"Keep goin', I'm listenin.'" He said as he and Michael laughed at her answer.

"He said that you would probably kill anybody that looked at you the wrong way and that's why people called you junkyard dog." She added as the waitress set her plate down.

"How long ago was he tellin' you all of this?" Douglas asked her.

"Probably two or three years ago but you don't forget stuff like that and that's why I've been scared of you." She said. "Do you carry a gun?"

"I used to carry a forty-five and that's the only thing that he said was true so put that other stuff out of your mind." "I take that back, I was junkyard dog but I've never killed anybody; I might've come close but that never happened."

"Then I remember him tellin' me that you had a different woman every week-end and he was actin' like he didn't do any of all that."

"So what was his point?" Michael asked her.

"Because he has his own issues and he was tryin' to make himself feel better." "But anyway, am I gonna get a lecture from you?" She asked Douglas.

"Do you feel like you need one?"

"I was just doin' what it takes to make it down here plus I love what I'm doin' so why not?" She said boldly. "And if I can't find a job up there that's any better than what I had down here, I might just come back down here and pick up where I left off."

"And take the chance of gettin' arrested again?"

"I would just have to take my chances but if you can get a good job, I can too so I might not have to do that." She said to Michael. "How did you do that so quick anyway?"

"It's a long story, I'll have to tell you about it." He said. "And I didn't do it, God did."

"Since when do you talk about God all of a sudden?" She asked him with sarcasm. "And it's somethin' different about the way you look dude."

"Is it really?" "If I told you about it, you wouldn't understand so I'm not gonna even try right now."

"What did you do, go up there and get religion or somethin'?"

"I didn't get religion, I got the Holy Ghost and there's a big difference."

Whatever Michael but I don't want any of this to get back to Doris or mother or anybody else in the family because I don't need to hear about it anymore."

"Why would we do that?" Douglas asked her.

"Because you can so I'm just makin' sure that this is our secret and I'm not sure if I'm done with that yet anyway, I have to do what I have to do.".

APRIL 24, FRIDAY

"Do you want to know or do you want us to keep it a secret from you?" The sonogram technician asked Janice Friday morning as she laid down on the table with Chris sitting next to her.

"I might as well find out, I need to know how to plan for stuff." She said after a moment.

"We need to know what color to paint your nursery." Chris told her.

She nodded a little as the technician raised her top and applied the gel.

"We can do that in just about a minute here." "Are you ready to hear the heartbeat too?"

She nodded again as she looked over at the screen in anticipation of the baby's image and became overwhelmed as the 4-D picture suddenly appeared and became apparent that its face was the exact one of Craig's.

"It looks just like him." She managed to say as memories of the life that she had left behind came flooding back in an instant.

"It's okay Janice." Chris said then as if to read her mind.

"And you have a baby girl on the way hon." The sonographer said a minute later after moving the instrument around to identify its gender. "Her heartbeat is strong and her development is right where it's supposed to be for sixteen weeks." She added as she continued to examine her. "So pink paint it is."

"This is almost scary Chris and every time I look at her, I'm gonna think about him and how he messed me over." Janice remarked half an hour later in the hospital cafeteria with Chris as she kept looking at the sonogram pictures.

"No you won't and if you do, just rebuke that thought and keep it movin.'" She told her as she opened her straw. "Are you gonna call your mother and tell her that she has a granddaughter on the way?"

"I knew you would ask me that and I really do need to get that over with don't I?"

"It won't be as bad as you think; don't magnify stuff in your mind because most of the time things like this work themselves out."

"I hope so because I've got other things I'm thinkin' and prayin' about." Janice said as she put the pictures in her purse.

"Michael?" Chris asked her.

She nodded. "How did you know?"

"I just sort of figured that was comin' and you're doin' the right thing by prayin' about it because if you jump into somethin' like that, it can end up bein' a mess if you're not careful."

"I was just really shocked because I thought that this baby would run a man off, you know what I mean?"

"Usually it does but every now and then, this happens and maybe this is one of those times where that doesn't matter." Chris said. "Does Douglas know that he's talked to you about it?"

"Before he said anything to me, he told him that he was gonna bring it up and he told him that he could fall as hard as he wanted to as long as we don't neglect our salvation." She said, amused.

"And that is so true Janice, please don't forget that." Chris told her. "I remember when James and me started to get really serious and this wasn't that long after he got the Holy Ghost."

"Yeah he told me how he had to put his brakes on because things were sort of goin' where they weren't supposed to."

"And you know it and I don't care how full of the Holy Ghost you might be, your flesh doesn't care." Chris said. "You have to keep it real because both of you are fresh out of the world and you're inexperienced when it comes to this so you have to set some boundaries, you know what I mean?" "And both of you have what it takes to keep you out of trouble but you have to allow your power to work."

"I don't have a problem with that but I do know that he's a man and like you said, we have to keep it real." Janice said. "I already know." She said as she thought about their incident.

"And that's why Douglas said not to neglect your salvation and that means stayin' prayed up and all of that other good stuff that we do." She said as she got a text alert from Irene.

"Is that Irene?" Janice asked.

She nodded. "She wants to know what the verdict is."

"Tell her I'll take all of the baby girl clothes she has and thanks for her support." She said.

"She said yay, you're savin' her a trip to Goodwill." Chris said a few moments later. "So everybody wins."

"How did you hook up with Irene's mother, that's strange." Terry remarked as she and Michael sat in his car after she finished with job applications.

"The day after I got here, I was ridin' around with Douglas doin' applications just like we did today and we stopped at her house." He began. "And as soon as she saw me walk in the door with him, she gave me this hug like she hadn't seen me in twenty years."

"You lyin' Michael, who does that?"

"She did and that was hard for me to understand but the longer I hung around these people around here, the more of that I saw and after a while, I was startin' to see what we've missed out on Terry."

"Just because we don't go around huggin' everybody all of the time doesn't mean that we're missin' out Michael." She came back. "Everybody's not into all of that and I just hope that you're not gettin' off into all of this church stuff and then find out that it's not what you thought it was."

"And that's what you don't understand, anybody can go to church but what happened to me almost a week ago doesn't have much to do with that." Michael said. "I had gotten to the place where I was doin' stupid stuff like drivin' around here and endin' up downtown with a D.W.I. on my record now and you know as well as I do, I don't do stuff like that."

"You didn't tell me that, when did that happen?" She asked him, surprised.

"Almost two weeks ago and I had to call Douglas to come and pay me out of there just like you did so now I know what that feels like."

"Did you get a lecture?"

"Not one word so you don't have any reason to be afraid of him and whatever David told you, try to put that mess out of your mind."

"It was like he had somethin' against him and he was tryin' to make me dislike him but if you say so." She said. "But tell me somethin', does Irene ever worry about other women goin' after him?"

"Somebody might try but they wouldn't get anywhere."

"How do you know Michael, he's a good lookin' guy with money and a position so you know somebody has tried."

"I don't get in his business like that but she doesn't worry about that, trust me."

"She's not that naïve is she?" Terry asked, becoming irritated with him. "It happens all of the time and I know he's all into the church thing but that don't mean nothin' anymore." She added. "If he wasn't my brother, I'd probably go after him and I could get him too." She said with bold confidence.

"Is that all you think about Terry?" Michael asked her after a moment.

"It's what you do Michael, what is with you?" She asked him. "Before you came up here, you kept a girlfriend and I know you wasn't just playin' house either."

"That was then and this is now." He said, shaking his head, refusing to be brought down by her conversation.

"Have you found anybody up here yet?"

"That's somethin' that you'll just have to wait and see about Terry, don't lose any sleep worryin' about it."

"I won't but I can see you climbin' the walls and takin' a lot of cold showers if you don't snap out of this whatever it is you're in dude." She told him. "And I can say that to you because I'm your sister and I'm just keepin' it real."

"And I've got some real power now to keep me out of trouble, believe me when I tell you ma'am."

"Yeah right Michael and I love you too."…

SUNDAY, APRIL 26

So how did your first week go for you, I haven't had a chance to get with you before now because it's been a pretty different week but I've been thinkin' a lot about you." Frances asked as Michael sat down with her Sunday evening in the kitchen.

"I can't think of the right word and I'm still tryin' to get used to myself because I'm not even thinkin' the way that I used to." He said. "It's a little unreal."

"But that's exactly what is supposed to happen honey, you have the mind of God now and it's totally different from what you're used to."

"Don't get me wrong, I'm lovin' it but it's still somethin' that's really blowin' my mind."

"Have you been talkin' to your brother about things that you might not understand?"

"Every day and every time I talk to him, I find out things that I didn't have any idea about and it's just good to have him around."

"It is but there's nothin' like findin' some time in the day for just you and the Lord to communicate too and believe me, He will talk to you when you learn how to listen." She said as she set a piece of cherry pie down on the table in front of him.

"That's deep too, this time two weeks ago, you couldn't have told me that I would be actually prayin' but it's workin.'"

"And just like it worked for you before it'll keep workin' for you and the more that you acknowledge God, the better off you'll be." Frances said as she sat back down. "That goes for everyday things and spiritual things too so don't ever be afraid to tell the Lord about all of it." "He already knows but He still wants to hear from you."

"James told me somethin' the other day and it's really crazy how other people can know just what to say and when to say it."

"What did he tell you?"

"We were workin' out at the lot one night last week and I don't even remember what were talkin' about but he told me about the scripture that tells you about havin' the desires of your heart."

"Psalms thirty-seven and verse four." Frances said as she immediately recognized what he was referring to. "Have you gotten yourself a bible yet?"

"Douglas has a couple of extra ones that I've been lookin' through 'til I can get one." He said. "And how did you know where to find that so quick like that?"

"Because I've been walkin' with the Lord for almost fifty years and it would be somethin' wrong if I didn't know where that scripture is." She said. "And when you get a chance, find that whole chapter and take it verse by verse and it pretty much covers anything that you can think of."

"When I get back home I'll do that and see how much of it I can really understand then I'll come back and give you a progress report."

"Just ask the Lord to open up your understanding of His word and that's why you make sure that you get to bible class every week because that's how you grow." Frances told him. "I told Janice the same thing and she hasn't missed one yet and I'm startin' to get the feelin' that she's startin' to be the desire of your heart isn't she?"

"Since it's you that asked me that, I don't have any choice but to be honest about it do I?"

"You could not tell the truth about it and your Holy Ghost would start to condemn you so you might as well be honest about it and there's not a thing wrong with that." She told him.

"I had a chance to talk to her Tuesday after the funeral and I could tell that she was pretty much in shock when I told her that I was interested in havin' more than a friendship with her, but like I told her, I'm serious, time is out for playin' around."

"And I know that you told Douglas that too didn't you?"

"You already know Aunt Frances because I realize how protective he is about her and he gave me some things to think about."

"Because he doesn't want to see her hurt again and when you take on somebody else's responsibility, it's not always easy."

"Chris told me that she's havin' a girl."

"And she said that she looks exactly like her father and that'll be a reminder of him but there's nothing that can be done about that." She said as she continued to "counsel" him. "But if you feel like that you're willin' to overlook all of that, then I would consider her to be definitely blessed."

"That works both ways and we're bein' really careful about this because we know it would be a permanent thing." Michael said. "That's one of the things that Douglas made sure that I knew, there's no such thing as gettin' a divorce just because you think you can't get along."

"And that's part of holiness because God hates divorce and there's just one reason that the scripture gives you to go there." Frances told him. "If one of you would break your vows and decide to get somebody on the side, then that's your only out."

"That's some serious stuff but when you think about it, if two people both have the Holy Ghost, why should it be such a problem to make it?" He asked. "I've been watchin' Chris and James since the first day that I met them and I know that it hasn't been that long, but to me, they really seem to have it together." "And that's not takin' anything away from Irene and Douglas either, they're somethin' else too." He added.

"Have you ever asked James and Chris how they do what they do?"

"I was talkin' to Chris one day and she told me that one of the reasons that they're so close is because they've run into so many people that want to see them fall out and split up because of the race thing and that's had the opposite effect; it's made 'em that more determined to make it."

"And I think that she's more colorblind than he is because he has a problem with his own, and I love him to death but he's got some issues that he's gonna have to let the Lord help him with." She said as they laughed together.

"But he's good to talk to, when Douglas is not around he told me to call him anytime I needed to."

"And that's a good thing because none of us make it through here without somebody else's help." Frances said. "There's so much goin' on that I never thought I'd live to see but that just lets us know how close we need to be to each other because you never know what the Lord will allow to happen from day to day because it's not gonna get any better."

"I can see that now because my eyes have come open about a lot of things so that's part of it too huh?"

"Honey you're catchin' on to what this is all about so don't listen to anybody that tells you that you're crazy or out of your mind or whatever else you might hear." Frances told him. "When God gave you his spirit, He gave you what the scrpture call a treasure and I don't care how tough things might get, never let the devil talk you into goin' back out there because that's a trick that can take you out of here without God and that's the worse way to go."

"Do you know anybody that has ever done that?" Michael asked her as he became thoroughly taken in by her words of wisdom.

"The man that we just buried a few days ago was one of the most faithful people that I had ever known but when things started to get a little tough, he started to question the Lord about some things and led to a lot of discouragement in his mind." She began as she recalled her experience with William.

"So what did he do, just say one day that he wasn't gonna do this anymore?"

"I remember it like it was yesterday but when people go back, it happens gradually." She said. "You start doin' things again that the Lord delivered you from, you'll stop comin' to church, you stop prayin' and get weak and before you know it, you're all the way back out there and there's no guarantee that you can get back."

Michael shook his head at the thought.

"But back to mister William, it was a Sunday mornin' and I had gotten the kids ready to go to Sunday school; I just happened to go out on the front porch, and he was sittin' there readin' the newspaper with a can of beer in his hand and a cigarette in his mouth and I about passed out because I was so shocked."

"Did you ask him what was goin' on?"

"He looked up at me and said from now on I'll be goin' to church by myself because he was done with all of that and he never went back." She said. "So from then on, it was up to me to make sure that me and the kids got there because I couldn't let what he was doin' or not doin' affect what I had to do because when it comes down to it, this is an individual thing."

"In other words, just because you change your mind about doin' the right thing doesn't give me an excuse to go back."

"Honey that is exactly right, I can tell that you're lettin' your Holy Ghost teach you some things." She told him as he allowed her to take his hand. "And if you never remember anything else that I tell you, I want you to listen to what the Lord just gave me for you." She said pausing. "I don't know what's comin' down your street but God does and because you're young and because all of this is new to you, you have to be taught or the devil will eat you alive if you don't have any knowledge."

"I'm hangin' on to every word that you're sayin', believe me."

"I would do your brother like this too right after he came out of the world and he needed some intensive care and love because this way of livin' was so totally opposite from what he came out of." Frances said, recalling her "talks" with Douglas. "James was different because he was like Chris, they grew up in this and have never known anything else but he was different, and once he started to get it, there was no goin' back." "He was determined to find out as much as he could about what he had been missin' out on and that's why he's so intense about what he says and does now, he's sold out and locked in."

"You got that right, sometimes when we're talkin' about things like this, I can almost feel his passion or whatever you want to call it and it's hard to ignore it, you know what I mean?"

"It's like that with him because he came so close to losin' his soul and it doesn't get any worse than that." She told him. "We talk about makin' it to heaven when Jesus comes and how wonderful it's goin' to be but there's another side to eternity that nobody likes to talk about but it's just as real baby."

"You don't like to think about it but it is." He said agreeing with her about the reality of hell.

"And there may be some times when your mind will tell you that you had it easier out there and livin' holy is not worth the trouble, and any other lie that the devil might put in your mind is just that; lies." "People are decieved every day because they listen to their own minds instead of what the Holy Ghost is telin' them."

"But why would you go back to that kind of craziness that doesn't do anything but mess you up in the long run?" "I'm not understandin' that."

"You probably don't understand that because you haven't been through anything yet but in the heat of a test, I'm not gonna lie to you and say that you won't be tempted to put your salvation on the shelf and come back to it later when you feel more like it." Frances said. "But that's a dangerous thing and because the Lord is so merciful, a lot of times, people will go back out there where the devil is doin' his best to kill you and then He'll help you come to yourself and realize what you had and bring you back like nothin' ever happened." She added. "But at the same time we can't take Him for granted either because mercy runs out and there's a place in the scripture that says it's like a dog goin' back to his vomit and crucifyin' the Lord all over again."

"Are you serious?" Michael asked her. "I actually saw a dog do that one time and I almost threw up myself after seein' it." He said laughing a little at the thought.

"In fact, it's better for you to have never known the Lord than to know what this is about and then go back to what God delivered you from." Frances said as she stirred a teaspoon of sugar in her cup of coffee. "But we were talkin' about you and your friend a few minutes ago, I don't how we got off track like that." She said then.

"But I'm glad that you did, that was some deep stuff you just laid on me and you know how to break it down so it's understandable." Michael said. "And as far as Janice goes, we decided that we're gonna pray about each other and see what happens."

"And that's the best thing that you can do right now, God sees the big picture with things and you can't go wrong by acknowledgin' Him because like we said before, marriage is permanent over here."

"Is that why I haven't seen a lot of problems around here that I always used to hear about from the guys that I used to hang out with in St. Louis?" He asked her. "They would always have these nightmare stories about how trapped they were and all the baby mama drama that was goin' on just made me not wanna be serious with anybody."

"That's the way the world does things but you're in a different place now." "What you've seen around here is proof that it can be done but it takes work and effort for it to be right."

"I'm just glad that I have some good examples because otherwise, I might be runnin' away from what I know is normal."

"It is and as long as both of you keep the right mindset, if it's to be, it'll happen and things will just fall into place." Frances told him. "Just keep believin' God."…

CHAPTER 2

APRIL 28, TUESDAY

"The only reason I took this job was because I can walk over there so once I get a car, I'll find somethin' that pays better." Terry told Irene Tuesday morning as she sorted clothes in the laundry room.

"One of us can pick you up at eleven, it's probably not a good idea for you to be out walkin' that late Terry." Irene told her.

"Don't you know I'm used to that, that's what I do." She said boasting. "But don't worry, nobody's gonna have to come and get me out of the slammer anymore, I won't do that to Michael and Douglas again." "Maybe." She added, laughing a little. "Where is he anyway, didn't he get off at seven?"

"He said he was goin' out to my brother's house for a couple of hours to do some painting, he said he'd be here by noon."

"How is he gonna be up all night and then go work somewhere else?" "He's gonna fall out if he keeps doin' that."

"He's like Douglas, neither one of 'em sleep that much; I noticed that the first week he was here."

"I'm gonna have to work him over about a couple of things when I see him because I'm seein' things that I don't like for him."

"Like what?" Irene asked her as she started the washer.

"He told me about your pregnant sister and how they decided to give it a try and I just don't understand it." She said. "How is he gonna even look at somebody that's already knocked up with somebody else's baby Irene?" "Is he crazy or what?"

25

"Honey he's not crazy, that evidently doesn't matter to him because I think he's dead serious."

"But that's not Michael, what happened to him in less than a month?"

"That's somethin' that you're gonna have to ask him, I wouldn't feel right tryin' to explain that but it is what it is." "He could tell that about her the first time he saw her and he might not understand it himself but I'm sure he knows how he feels."

"He thinks he knows, that's why I'm gonna have to get in his head and straighten him out."

"When did he tell you about her?"

"We were talkin' last night right before he left to go to work and he wanted to let me know about her before I actually met her so I wouldn't be surprised."

"You're probably not gonna be able to change his mind."

"Yeah I will, and she needs to know that I'm not sharin' him with anybody and if I can't help him out, all I have to do is let David know what's goin' on."

"Is he still in Kansas City?"

"He moved back to St. Louis about a year ago and I would've called him the other night but he might've chewed me up and spit me out big time so I didn't bother him." She said after a moment. "So Michael needs to wake up or he's gonna be in a trap that he can't get out of." "And you heard it from me first."

APRIL 30, THURSDAY

"She might not even look like this by the time she's born but right now, she looks exactly like him." Janice remarked Thursday evening as she and Michael sat on the porch after dinner.

"And that's botherin' you too, I can tell."

"It is because when I look at this, it just reminds me of that other life, you know what I mean?" She asked him as she handed him the sonogram pictures.

"But you can look at this two ways, if this hadn't happened, you wouldn't be here with the testimony that you have." He told her. "You can help somebody else now and you never know who you're gonna run into so don't be surprised when you get the chance."

She nodded a little as she thought about how close she had come to "taking care of the problem" but because of the all knowing mind of God, her circumstances were forever changed.

"Do you feel like walkin' around the block a couple of times?" He asked her then. "Chris told me to keep you active."

"I'm not keepin' you from anything else am I?" She asked him as they started walking down the block a minute later.

"I'm off tonight so I don't have to be anywhere 'til I pick Terrry up tonight from the store at eleven."

"When am I gonna get to meet her?"

"I'll check with her and see when she's off and I'll work somethin' out."

"So is she here to stay for a while or is she goin' back to St. Louis?"

"If she can find a job up here that's better than what she had down there, I can see her stayin' because she's crazy about her brothers."

"How does that make you feel?"

"In a way it's a little flattering but when she starts to get possessive, it turns into somethin' else that can cause problems."

"Is she the youngest?"

"She is and you know what they say about the youngest, they're used to havin' their way and when they don't, it's a problem."

"I don't know what that's like, Marie was always the one that got her way and now I know why but that just doesn't matter anymore."

"You know what I'm gonna ask you don't you?" Michael asked her.

"Yeah I do and I actually called her Saturday to tell her that I'm havin' a girl and it was like nothin' ever happened." Janice said, shaking her head a little. "It's like she's in some kind of denial but if that's how she's dealin' with it, then I won't bring it up either."

"There you go soundin' like you're thirty instead of eighteen."

"That's what happens when you hang around people that have some sense, they rub off on you."

"And it can work the other way around too, I almost got mixed up with some guys in St. Louis that would go out and get high every Friday after work." He recalled. "And I decided to hang out with 'em one week-end and the first time I tried to smoke a joint, I got sicker than a dog." He recalled. "And they kept tellin' me that the more I did it, the easier it would be and I listened to what they were tellin' me because it was the thing to do."

"Then before you know it, you're addicted to it and can't stop yourself?"

"That's how it happens but I had enough sense to know not to let it get that far but that's how Douglas got hooked on it." He told me he tried it once and it kept gettin' easier to do and before he knew it, he was usin' it and sellin' it too."

"He needs to write a book or somethin', he could help a lot of people just by talkin' about what the Holy Ghost did for him."

"Tell him that and he might go for it." He still sees people that he used to run around with and they can't believe that he's livin' like he is."

"Because people expect you to mess up and when they see that you're really serious, they don't like it." Janice said as they turned the corner. "I'm workin' next to somebody that doesn't wanna believe that James and me don't have anything goin' just because we come and go at the same time." "They think this baby is his and all kind of crazy stuff is goin' on to try to catch me off guard but I'm learnin' how to start prayin' for people like that."

"So what does he have to say about that?"

"He just kind of ignores the things that they're sayin' because he knows if he ever got started, he might say somethin' off so he doesn't say anything at all and they hate it."

"Do you think it's because of the race thing?"

"That might have somethin' to do with it and James really has a problem with his people anyway if you know what I mean."

"He said somethin' one time that I thought was kind of different but I didn't know that." Michael remarked. "We were talkin' about how Jane's mother came through for them and he said somethin' like they're not all bad and I could tell that he's strugglin' a little bit about that."

"He is and he wasn't like that until his mother turned on Chris but I told him if he doesn't watch that it'll turn into hate."

"I just love the way you tell it like it is Janice, where do you get it like that?"

"You already know, I'm sayin' things now that I wouldn't have even thought about but this is Holy Ghost stuff, can't help it."

"Just like you couldn't keep yourself from doin' the wrong stuff now it's the other way around huh?"

"Somethin' like that and the more I sit and listen to Aunt Frances talk about stuff, the more I understand things."

"My best friend." "I could sit and listen to her all day long and I'll be glad when I can help somebody else like she does."

"When I first moved here, I thought she was out of touch when she would talk about doin' things God's way but some things don't change."

"And because things are so crazy now, you really don't have much of a choice if you expect to make it." He said as his phone vibrated.

"Where you at Michael?" Terry asked him after he answered.

"I'm with Janice, why?" He asked cautiously.

"I need for you to help me get a car so I won't have to walk everywhere around here."

"Do you have anything to put down on one?"

"I don't get paid for another two weeks but I called this place I found on line and all they need is a thousand dollars down or you can go with me and tell 'em that we're married so they can use your income too."

"You're not serious are you?"

"Yeah I'm serious, I need a car." She insisted. "You don't want me to start walkin' around here do you?" "I can get that in a week but I know Douglas would make me go back to St. Louis if he found out."

"No he wouldn't, he'd probably loan you the money before he would do that."

"I'm not doin' that when all I have to do is hook up with a couple of guys on my job that know what I do and it wouldn't be a problem." She said. "And I'm tryin' to stay out of trouble but if you won't do that, I guess I don't have a choice." She said in a matter of fact way.

"Let me talk to Douglas before you do that, that's not necessary." He told her.

"Just lie and tell him that it's for you, he won't know the difference."

"You really don't know him do you?"

"All I know is that I need a car and I'll do whatever I need to do to get one."

"I'll call you back, where are you, at work?"

"I'm on my lunch break, call me back before eight."

"You weren't expectin' to see me here were you?" Douglas asked Terry after she got in the car with him around eleven o' clock after she got off work at the store.

"Did Michael call you?"

"He did and I think that you're startin' to find out that he's different from what he was in St. Louis." He told her. "He won't be doin' the same stuff that he was involved in down there so that's somethin' that you have to get used to."

"Just because he's all into what's her name, he can't help me out when I need it?" She asked him, becoming irritated.

"Janice doesn't have anything to do with what we're talkin' about so leave her out of this." He said after a moment. "So if you need money to get a car, nobody has to do anything under the table for that to happen."

"So you're tellin' me you have it like that and I can get it from you without havin' to bother Michael with it?"

"If he had it, he'd probably be glad to help you out but he just got a new job and he's not in a place where he can be doin' that right now."

"Then how is he gonna be tryin' to be stuck with her and somebody else's baby Douglas?" "That's crazy, he can do all that for her but he can't help me out?"

"Honey what did I just say a second ago?" "This is between you and me and Michael, there's no reason for you to keep puttin' her in this." He firmly told her.

"Then you know what Douglas, I can take care of this myself and I know that I don't have to draw you any pictures."

"And because you have your own mind and I can't stop you from doin' what you're determined to do, it's you that'll have to deal with your decisions."

"So you're sayin' that you don't care that I might have to do some work on the side to get it faster?"

"I care more than you'll ever know but I have enough sense to realize that you're gonna do what you want to do, regardless of how I feel about it." He told her. "And if I thought that givin' you a thousand dollars would help you get a car, I would write you a check tonight to keep you from goin' there but I'm not that naïve sweetheart."

"I never said that you were naïve Douglas but I wouldn't feel right takin' any money from you." She said. "You've got six kids and Irene's not workin' and she would probably get mad at me for takin' it so I'll figure somethin' else out."

"That's not for you to worry about and that's not the issue anyway." He said. "I'm more concerned about you riskin' your life on the street because I've been out there and it's worse now than it was then."

"But I'm not just doin' it for the money, I do it because I like it and I'm keepin' it real with you because I think you understand where I'm comin' from." She told him.

"I do understand where you're comin' from which is why I can talk to you like I'm about to." He told her with unconstrained boldness. "If you keep doin' what you're doin, you're playin' with your life and your soul and believe me when I tell you, it's not worth it."

"I know how to take care of myself Douglas so don't try to scare me out of anything." She promptly told him.

"And if and when somethin' happens, we'll be here for you because we love you so don't ever feel like you can't come to us for help." He told her as he purposely ignored her last comment but continued to give her what he had received through intercessory prayer for her.

"This is somethin' that I can't help Douglas and since I can't stop it, I just make the most out of it, you know what I'm sayin'?" She asked him after a moment.

"I know what you're sayin' but how long have you been lettin' men use you up like this?"

"A couple of years because that's when I started to need more money than what I was makin' on my job and that was the easiest way to get it." She admitted. "I've had to get a couple of abortions because I guess I wasn't careful enough but that just comes along with it."

"I'm not askin' for any details like that Terry but if you're willin' to let us help you with this, then that's half the battle." "If you really feel like you need to stop what you're doin', you can and you will be delivered from this." He spoke with authority.

"Why does it matter to you what I do Douglas?" She asked him after a moment.

"It matters to me because what you're doin' can eventually take you out of here and has anybody ever told you that you have a soul?"

"Maybe." She said, shrugging a little.

"What does that mean to you?"

"I've never really thought about it Douglas, you know that they didn't make us go to church." She said, referring to their parents.

"I know they didn't, which was why I ended up doin' any and everything that I thought I was big enough to do and I almost lost my life out there." He told her. "I was one of those guys that would pick up women on the street, do my thing and move on to the next one but what I didn't realize was that I have a soul that needed salvation." "All of that stuff I got involved in was killin' me everyday and it wasn't until I saw instant death happen right next to me, that I figured it out."

"You saw somebody die?"

"One second we were talkin' about drug deals and the next thing I knew, his body was in two pieces, right there in front of me." He said, recalling the experience. "I tell people about that every chance that God gives me because it wasn't anything but His mercy that it wasn't me and what you don't want to do is to take that for granted because none of us is promised the next minute."

"I know that and if I die, I die Douglas." She told him. "I really have tried to stop this but it's not as easy as it might seem."

"And that's why you need the help and power of God to deliver you from this." He told her again. "And this is somethin' that you have to decide for yourself, and if you want help bad enough, it's there and you just told me that if you die, you just die, didn't you?"

She nodded.

"Has anybody ever taken the time to tell you that your soul never dies?" He asked her.

She shook her head as she kept looking ahead of her.

"This body that you and me are livin' in is gettin' older everyday and one day, it's gonna check out of here if the Lord doesn't come first but your soul is gonna be in Eternity in one of two places and you can't gamble with it."

"Did you talk to Michael like this?" She asked him.

"Irene's mother latched on to him before I got the chance to but he got to the place where he hit rock bottom and he went to see her one day and somethin' clicked." "I don't know what all she said to him but he didn't put up a fight with his soul, he knew when he was licked and when he gave himself up, that's when God took over and kept His promise to give him the Holy Ghost and that's why he's so different from what you're used to."

"So does he think that he's better than me now or somethin'?"

"Of course not Terry, he's still your brother and he still loves you and all of that but don't ask him to do anything dishonest or somethin' that might get him in trouble because he's not goin' there anymore."

"Whatever Douglas and I might try to remember some of the stuff that you said but like I said, this is somethin' that I can't stop myself from doin', like it or not."

"And when it's like that, nothin' or nobody but God can help you if you want it." Douglas told her. "And in the sight of God, one thing is no worse than the other; with me it was drugs and alcohol, but whatever it might be, it's not too big or hard for the Lord to take it away from you."

"Are you gonna pray for me?" She asked him in a half way joking manner.

"As long as I feel like you can be helped, absolutely but don't get to the place where the Lord won't deal with you anymore." "He won't force His help on you but if you keep doin' your own thing, He will allow the devil to take you out of here and it's happenin' to people everyday."

Again she nodded a little in acknowledgement.

"And if you need me to help you get a car, I can do that and you don't have to worry about Irene gettin' mad at you, I know how to take care of business."

"So what do I have to do to pay you back?"

"Don't worry about that right now, we'll talk about it later but I need to let you know that the things I've said to you tonight are for your good." He began. "And if you don't remember anything else, get yourself out of the way and let God help you."…

MAY 2, SATURDAY

"This is going to be absolutely gorgeous, you have a lot of talent young man." Jane's mother Florence remarked Saturday morning as she and James walked through he and Chris' new house.

"This is basically the same floor plan as the house we're leavin' but the rooms are bigger." James said as they started back down the steps to the lower level.

"And how big is your family?"

"There's gonna be eleven of us in here with one on the way so I had to make sure that we have enough room to spread out."

"And when do you expect to actually move in?"

"It'll be another two or three weeks, they still have a few other things that need to be done before it's inspected and all of that so we'll be in here by the end of the month."

"I would love to meet your wife, do you ever bring her out here to keep her up on things?"

"She was out here last week, she really wanted to see how the kitchen came together in here." James said as they approached it.

"Oh this is perfect, did she pick out the countertops and the color scheme and everything?" She asked him as she walked around inspecting the work.

"She did, it really didn't make me that much difference what she decided to do, this is her house so she's the boss."

"Have you hired a good housekeeper yet?" "If you don't have anybody in mind yet, I have a list of girls that I have known for years that would love to work in a house like this."

"No way." James said shaking his head. "Do people still do that?"

"Not so much anymore but back when I was raising Jane, just about every household that could afford it had a girl that would come in once or twice a week to do the laundry and dusting or whatever needed to be done." She said.

"I guess I'm not old enough to remember that but I've heard about mess like that."

"Why do you call it mess, that's why they were brought here, for us." She said as she detected his disgust. "And this is why Jane's father and I were so shocked and appalled when she married Paul and I really don't think it would've turned out that way if she hadn't started going to that church that's so integrated."

"Are you still havin' a problem with that?" James asked her as he felt a spirit of anger rise up in him.

"I don't exactly agree with it but I know now that he loves her and they have all of these children together so I'm trying to make the best of it." She said after a moment. "Her father wouldn't have done this for them but I'm in control now and if it helps her in any way, I have to do it."

He nodded a little while keeping himself from judging her for her comments.

"And I wanted to meet you out here because I have something for you." She said as she sat her purse down on the island. "I want you and your wife to have this because you're doing such a wonderful job with Jane and Paul's house over there and I feel like you deserve it."

She said as she handed him a cashier's check for twenty-five thousand dollars. "I don't need to hear you say thank-you or anything like that because what you're doing over there for my daughter is pretty phenominal."

"Did you know that I'm married to Paul's sister?" He asked her as he reluctantly took the check from her. "And this is her's." He added as he watched the color drain from her face.

"I'm a little disappointed by that but what's done is done." She managed to say as she turned to walk out of the house. "You have a good day young man."

"How many times have you heard me say that God is not gonna be outdone?" Douglas remarked as he and James sat out on the screened porch later that evening. "This is pretty awesome."

"I don't feel right takin' it so this is Chris' money, I don't want anything to do with it."

"Because it came from her?"

"After I told her that I was married to Pauls' sister, I could tell right away how sorry she was but it was too late, she wasn't gonna ask for it back."

"So how did that come up?"

"Jane called and told me that she wanted to meet me out there this mornin'so I'm thinkin' okay, she wants to see how we're doin' on the house, I didn't think that much about it." He began. "So we got done walkin' through their house and she wants to go through ours too so I'm easy, we can do that."

"I smell a rat."

"Then she asked me if we had hired a housekeeper and I guess she could tell that that was rubbin' me the wrong way." He continued. "But when she made this comment about that was why they were brought over here, to work for us, that's when I really went south with her." He admitted. "I'm confessin', so help me out."

"I am, keep goin.'" Douglas told him.

"And she went on about how shocked and messed up her and Jane's father were when she married Paul and the more she talked, the worse it got." "I almost took her by her arm and escorted her out of there because I was so ticked off, so this is gettin' worse instead of better."

"But if you let that happen, it would be just as bad or worse than what you heard from her because you're the one that has the power to overcome that stuff that your flesh wants to do." Douglas told him. "She probably has no idea how ignorant that stuff is and it almost makes me feel sorry for people like that."

"I've talked to Jane about this before and she's gotten to that place but it'll be a minute before I get there because right now, it's borderin' on some self hatred issues."

"Because you're what you are?"

"When I look at the way history has been, it almost makes me ashamed to be what I am and I'm not sayin' that to try to sound liberal or any of that crap either." He said as he continued to purge himself.

"But God doesn't make mistakes and we're not supposed to be puttin' all the emphasis on this flesh anyway." Douglas said a moment later after digesting what he had said. "Your Holy Ghost is to keep your spirit in the right place, not for this what you see that's basically dyin' everyday so it's secondary." He added as he took hold of his arm. "In other words, this skin that we're in is not where it's at and I know that you realize that but sometimes, we all need reminders about stuff because none of us has made it yet." He concluded.

"No good thing in it huh?" James said.

"That's the book and because the Lord is color blind, we'd better be." He said. "And I know that it's hard sometimes for us to love people like that but what choice do we have James?" "We're not gonna go out here and cheat on our wives but if we're not lovin' people like God does, we're in trouble."

"Are you sure that you haven't missed your callin'?" James asked him then.

"Man don't go there with me." Douglas said, shaking his head. "Somebody else said somethin' like that to me a couple of weeks ago but I'm not feelin' that, I'm just tellin' it like it is and tryin' to keep it real because I don't want to see you be consumed with stuff like this that the devil uses to throw us off track." He added. "And how long have you had this hangin' over your head like this?"

"I was on the borderline with 'em back when I was in high school and that might've been some of the reason that I was attracted to Chris." He began. "And then when my mother pulled that stunt with me that Christmas, I was done, no joke."

"But it's startin' to really come to a head now huh?"

"Seriously and I really have to catch myself because if it gets any worse, I might have to go back to the altar.' He said, laughing a little.

"That doesn't hurt anybody and just because I might not have your issue, I might have somethin' else so don't think that I'm judgin' you about anything, because the day might come when the tables are turned."

"Have I ever seen you with any kind of issue Douglas?"

"Just because you haven't seen much doesn't mean they're not there." He answered. "And sometimes I think I might be too hard on myself because of where the Lord brought me from, and I'm so determined not to let Junkyard out of his cage with the help of God, that I don't give myself an inch."

"Cause it'll take a mile as mother says." He said, imitating Frances.

"Sometimes two or three and when Kathryn did her thing that night, I was this close to losin' the fight with that spirit in her but it just pointed up to me that when you have the Holy Ghost, you have the greater over anything that tries to take you out." Douglas said as he recalled the incident with her.

"And I think when Janice saw her do that, somethin' clicked in her that helped her to know that this is real and not just a lot of talk."

"And that's another thing that we have to remember, we're bein' watched and scrutinized by people that're fed up with a lot of talk." Douglas remarked. "And I'm not sure how much of a difference that made to her but the outcome is what matters, she got her help, and I'm lovin' how much she's matured in God."

"We can really see it because she's in the house with us and it's like night and day from when we picked her up at the airport three months ago." James said. "And she told Chris the other day that she wants to eventually teach Sunday school in the primary department because she remembers how much the kids talked about it and it made more of a difference to her than she thought."

"That's my girl, I love it." Douglas said, "And you'll be alright too, so don't sweat it, just add your new friend to your prayer list because it sounds like she needs it." "You might be surprised at how that'll change your attitude about her."

"I can't forget the look on her face after I told her who I was married to and maybe I shouldn't have said anything but it was one of those things that was hard to resist." James said. "And after I told her that I was givin' this money to her, she called it disappointing but she knew that she couldn't take it back."

"Does Chris know about it yet?"

"I haven't been home yet and I might hold on to it 'til we move and surprise her with it."

"Do you think you'll be able to keep it for that long?"

"I'll put it in the bank and right before we actually move in there, I'll let her know about it." He said as Terry and Michael came in from outside.

"James, right?" She asked as she sat down.

"Yes ma'am, somebody's been talkin' about me."

"We just came from the lot, we went through your house because the door was open." Michael told him.

"I must've just missed you, I was out there this mornin' too."

"That's a tough place, when are you movin' in?" She asked him as she leaned towards him in a suggestive and provocative manner.

"Probably the first week in June, it's not quite finished yet." James said as he got up to leave. "Did I tell you that we got all of the rooms painted Friday?" He asked Michael, referring to Paul and Jane's house.

"Good deal, what's next?"

"We're pickin' up the kitchen cabinets probably Monday or Tuesday and that'll take two trips so if you're available, meet us out there around four thirty after I get off from work." He added as they walked out together.

"Tell me that you didn't see what I saw." Michael said a moment later as they approached the driveway.

"I saw what you saw which is why I'm out here and if we saw it, you know Douglas did."

"And he might be in there lettin' her have it too and if I had known that you were here, we would've found somewhere else to go, believe me." Michael told him.

"She's never seen me before in her life, what's up with that?"

"James, with her, that doesn't matter, that's what she does and Douglas talked to her the other night and she told him that she actually can't help herself." Michael said, shaking his head. "And I'm tryin' to be really careful here because I remember that move that I made with Janice and I had seen her what, once or twice?"

"I see what you're sayin' but Janice is not married with seven kids either. James said.

"That's what I'm sayin', with her, things like that don't matter because the world has gone crazy and anything and everything goes." Michael said. "And I've had the Holy Ghost a whole month now and I can't tell you how much my mind has changed about so much stuff."

"Has anybody got a chance to talk to her about that since she's been here?" James asked him.

"Douglas has but until she wants help, it's goin' in one ear and out the other, you know what I mean?" Michael said. "And when I get the chance, I'm gonna let her know that we know what's goin' on and there's no chance that you're goin' there with her."

"And you know it but don't run her away from where she can get help." "There's a way to do it without comin' off like you think you're better than she is but she needs to know that that doesn't fly here."

"I need to go talk to my best friend, this is botherin' me." Michael said then, as he thought about Frances. "Douglas is too close to it to be objective so I need another viewpoint."

"He is too close to it but I just got through dumpin' on him about my own issues so we don't go through here without somebody else's help so go back in there and start lovin' your sister to God." James told him. "And I'm goin' home to my wife and kids that I don't know what I'd do without so go do what you have to do too." "This'll be alright."

"Now do you see what I'm talkin' about Douglas?" Terry asked him as she sat across from him, still on the porch. "I really didn't mean to come off like that but that's what I'm used to doin.'" She said shrugging a little. "Do you think I should apologize to him?"

"I really don't think he's expectin' that from you Terry but let me ask you somethin.'" He said."Come over here for a minute, I don't bite."

"Are you about to whip me or somethin'?" She asked him cautiously. "I know I deserve it so I don't need a lecture from you." She added as she got up.

"When was the last time you got a hug from somebody?" He asked her a moment later after disregarding her last comment as she sat down next to him.

She couldn't answer as she struggled to remember any incidents of affection towards her.

"How does that make you feel?" Douglas asked her as he allowed her silence to confirm what he had believed to be true.

"I don't know because you don't miss what you've never really had Douglas." She finally told him. "So sometimes I do what I do because it makes me feel wanted, even if it's just for a couple of hours, it's better than nothin' at all." She continued as he allowed her to empty out. "You used to do drugs so you know what it feels like when you needed to get high, you did what you had to do to get that fix, even if you knew that it was just for a minute and even when you knew that it was wrong." "And if you think I should apologize to James I will, because it just happened before I knew what I was doin'; it's like men are some kind of magnet or somethin' and I know that sounds crazy or sick to you but it is what it is."

"I'm not gonna say that you're sick or crazy because like you said, I used to be in a place where you are and I know what it feels like." Douglas told her. "But I also know what those men are doin' to you because I've been there too and sooner or later, it'll catch up with you and you don't want to get there Terry." "And when you get to the place where you get fed up with it, God is your help, and that's the best way that I can explain it to you right now."

She nodded a little. "Do you think that God is gonna punish me because of the way I am?" She asked him.

"Honey I'm not in a place to say what the Lord will do because He's the only one that knows your heart and I'm not your judge." He immediately told her. "But I will tell you that He promised His spirit as a gift to you but you have to get to the place where you want and need His help." "And He's not going to force Himself on you but you're in eternal trouble without Him."

"So that's why Michael is so different?" "I don't even know him anymore."

"He's still your brother and all of that and he still loves you but he won't be doin' and actin' the same way that you're used to."

"Yeah I'm gettin' the message." She said with a resentful air in her voice. "Did he tell you that he's lookin' for an apartment?"

"He did because he doesn't want you to be crowded out and he knew that this was temporary when he first moved up here." He told her. "So don't feel like he's tryin' to get away from you or anything like that, it's a guy thing."

"So is Janice whatever her name is movin' in with him?" She asked.

"Not happenin', that's the kind of thing that he doesn't do anymore so it's almost like you're startin' all over with him." Douglas told her.

She nodded again and stood up to walk back into the house." "So can I get a hug Douglas?' She asked him. "I sort of need it."

"Absolutely and if you need to talk some more, you know where we live."…

CHAPTER 3

MAY 4, MONDAY

Man how long has it been since I've had the priviledge of talkin' to mister top dog himself?" David asked on the phone with Douglas Monday evening.

"Don't start with that, what's goin' on?" He asked him.

"You tell me, I've been talkin' to Terry about a few things and I can't believe that you're puttin' up with her stuff man, I'm pretty much in a state of shock."

"Why is that?"

"This girl is a promiscuous slut and she's livin' in your house probably sneakin' men in there when you're not home and you're askin' me why?" He asked. "Get real would you?"

"Question for you." Douglas told him after a moment.

"I'm all ears man, tell me somethin.'" "From what I hear about you, you went and got deep into the church thing and somehow, there's somethin' wrong with that picture."

"I know exactly what she's about so you're not tellin' me anything that I don't know but back to my question David." Douglas told him. "If I come home one day and find her in the bed with two or three men, what does that have to do with you?" He asked him. "What are you doin' to try to help her?"

"Did she happen to tell you about the two abortions that I had to help her pay for?"

"Actually she did and it's a heartbreaking thing so how do you live with yourself for havin' anything to do with that man?" Douglas asked him without reservation. "Those were two lives that you helped her get rid of and don't misunderstand me, I don't condone anything that she's doin' but if you would take the time to talk to her, you might be able to see the root of her problems."

"Is she givin' you some crap about not feelin' loved and all of that mess?" David threw at him. "I've heard it all dude and she has a way of talkin' her way out of stuff and if you fall for it, you're less than the man I thought you were mister big shot on the hill."

"So what is your point of all of this, I don't have time to waste arguin' about somethin' that doesn't have anything to do with you." Douglas calmly told him then. "Everything that you've said in the last few minutes is not news to me so is there somethin' else you need for me to know?"

"What is this about Michael and his pregnant girlfriend?" David asked him. "It's goin' from bad to worse."

"And Michael is seven times three plus some so that's somethin' you'll have to talk to him about." Douglas told him. "There is no way that you're gonna be able to get me caught up in a lot of confusion because I'm not about that David and if you have a problem with it, I don't know what else to tell you." He said as he began to defuse the conversation that was escalating by the minute. "And I don't know what Terry has told you but that's between the both of you too."

"You know what man, I'm gonna have to come up there and see for myself what's goin' on because you're out to lunch dude." "The next time you hear from me, it's gonna be face to face so take that as your warnin', time is out for this crap."..

MAY 6, WEDNESDAY

"I don't know why we didn't think about this before but it makes sense." James remarked at the closing table with Chris, Randy and Donna on Wednesday morning.

"Is she willin' to just walk away from that house that she's lived in for almost forty-five years though?" Randy asked him.

"That's the problem, there's too much that needs to be done to the house and she's sixty –five years old and doesn't need the headache of tryin' to fix it up." James said. "And since she's willin' to move out there with us, we have more than enough room for her and we're talkin' about two or three weeks from now."

"When Paul asked her about it, she wanted to know what took us so long to bring it up so it's just a matter of her packin' up whatever she wants to bring with her." Chris said. "She's all for it."

"And since she owns it outright, there's no mortgage to worry about, all she has to do is leave it and we we're wonderin' if Michael might want it." James said as the bank officers walked into the room. "Hold that thought."

"If this is not a God thing, I don't know what is." Michael remarked later that evening sitting with Paul, James and Frances in her breakfast nook.

'Talk about it, we're listenin.'" Paul told him.

"I think I've been around to five or six apartment complexes around here and every last one of 'em have told me that I haven't had this job long enough to get a place." He began. "And one thing that I learned right here in this house was that God answers prayer and I kept rememberin' what you told me." He told Frances.

"And you took that problem to the throne which is what the Lord wants you to do." She said as she noticed him respond to the presence of God around him.

"So this is the deal then." Paul said. "When James and Chris move out there in a couple of weeks, you'll just leave here and move in with them, Randy and Donna move in their place and Michael you'll take over this house after Sheila and Ruth leave and get their own place."

"Okay, back up, I'm confused." Michael said, laughing at him.

"What it is, is that Chris and me are technically homeless right now, we closed this mornin' so we're livin' in Donna and Randy's house til ours gets ready and it's almost there." James said. "So when we leave, she's movin' out of here and goin' with us and if you want this house, it's yours after Ruth and Sheila leave and everybody's happy."

"Have they already said that they don't want this place?" Michael asked. Suppose they wanna stay here, then it's no deal."

"They're already lookin' for an apartment to rent together so they know what's goin' on." Frances said. "And this house needs a lot of work done to it which is why I'll sell it to you for a dollar so I can say that I sold it to you instead of givin' it to you."

"That way, you can flip it and make it the way you want it." Paul told him. "The money that you would've paid to rent an apartment somewhere can go into fixin' up this place."

"A dollar?" Michael asked in shock.

"You heard me honey and we've been talkin' about this behind your back for about a week so the Lord is two steps ahead of you." Frances told him. "I want this house to stay in the family so you're the one that gets the prize for workin' so hard on Paul and Jane's place like you have."

"Are you sure that Ruth and Sheila don't want it?" He cautiously asked again.

"They're all for this so don't worry about them and as soon as I get that dollar from you, this'll be a done deal." She told him.

"Too much sugar for a nickle huh?" James asked him.

"Yeah pretty much and I'm tryin' to process this, give me a second." He said, shaking his head.

"Before we do this, I want you to read somethin' for me because I want you see how God works when you learn how to trust Him." Frances told him as she opened her bible that was sitting on the table. "And this is just one verse but it'll save you a lot of worry and stressin' out if you really believe it and let it get into your spirit son." She continued as she showed him the scripture.

"But my God shall supply all of your need according to His riches in glory by Christ Jesus." Michael read.

"And that's what He's doing for you so stop worryin' about it and just add this to your list of testimonies." Frances told him.

"Does anybody else know about this?" He asked as he sat there still trying to absorb what was happening.

"We all know about it, you're the last one to find out." Paul told him. "And we're doin' this because we found out that you've been goin' out to the house and workin' by yourself after bein' up all night on your job, and it's things like that that need to be rewarded, you know what I'm sayin'?"

"About all I've done is paint walls because I don't know how to do much else yet." He said with an humble spirit.

"For somebody that doesn't have a lot of experience, you've done a good job and whatever you've picked up out there will help you fix this place up like you want it." James said.

"Do you need some time to think about it or do you need me to go in there and get the deed and sign it over to you right here on the spot?" Frances asked him.

"You have to sign it in front of a notary mother, it's a little more complicated than that." Paul told her. "You're gonna have to go to the bank together so they can witness your signatures and all of that before it's a done deal."

"Would you feel more comfortable with this if I get an inspector over here so we can find out just how much you might have to do before you sign on the dotted line?" James asked him.

"That might be a good thing to do because the last thing I want to do is have you bite off more than you can chew honey so why don't you do that James, I'll pay for it." Frances told him.

"I'll get one out here tomorrow and we'll go from there but goin' from just what I can see, it'll be worth it, you're gonna come out on top." James told Michael then as he looked through the contact list on his phone.

"Sounds like a plan, you're not gonna get any argument from me." Michael said.

"This is what happens when you think about other people before you do yourself and that's what you've been doin' so just thank God and go on." Paul told him.

"So do you have a timeline on when their house is gonna be ready?" Michael asked James.

"If the weather stays like this, we should be done in another month and that'll be here in no time so basically, we're gonna be movin' out there at the same time." James said. "Chris is already throwin' a lot of stuff out and they might get a garage sale goin' between now and then." "You have to start somewhere."…

MAY 8, FRIDAY

"I had to come and see for myself how the other half lives and I didn't tell Douglas that I was comin' today but here I am." David remarked on Friday afternoon as he and Irene sat at the kitchen table.

"He told me that you called the other day but he'll be surprised that you're here." Irene said as she shook a baby bottle of milk before starting to feed Annette.

"And he must be takin good care of you, you're lookin' like a million bucks lady." He commented as continued to look around.

"He's definitely been a blessin, I have to give it to him. She admitted. "One of my cousins was here about a month ago and she told me not to take him for granted and ever since she told me that, I really don't."

"So what is Michael doin' with himself, Terry told me some stuff that worries me and that's part of the reason I came up here to see what's goin' on." He said with aggrevation in his voice. "Since mister can't do no wrong Douglas won't talk, maybe you will." He added in an attempt to intimidate her.

"Michael's doin' really good right now and that's because a few things happened after he first got here that sort of rocked his world, and he learned what God can do when he found out that he couldn't change things himself." Irene told him after she thought a moment. "But he can talk for himself and he should be here pretty soon if you can wait around for him."

"I'll let him know that I'm in town and maybe he'll show up a little quicker." David said as he began to text him. "But I'm here to tell both of you that you're playin' with fire by lettin' Terry stay here and where is she anyway?"

"She's at work, she doesn't get off 'til ten tonight."

"Workin' where, are you sure about that?" He asked her with skepticism. "And I don't know how much she's told you about herself but the girl has a serious problem and it's not gonna stop just because she moved up here with the corn fields."

"We know all about it David, calm down." She told him.

"Sweetheart how can you tell me to calm down when she's probably out there doin' anything and everything that you can think of for a some quick bucks." He came back with disgust. "I am so afraid for her and if you get a phone call one night that she's in the hospital or layin' up dead somewhere, you won't be able to say that you weren't warned." He said as Douglas came up the steps and into the kitchen.

"Hey man, back up, we don't talk about death in here." He told him as he approached him for a quick embrace after he stood up.

"Am I really in the presence of the king of the hill himself?" David asked him.

"Don't go there, that's the best way to shut me down." He told him. "Everything alright in here?" He asked as he turned his attention towards Irene after overhearing David's remarks a moment before.

"She's good, I just got through tellin' her how well you must be takin' care of her." He said, trying to "cover" himself.

"So how long have you been here?" Douglas asked him as he sat down next to Irene.

"Just a couple of hours ago and I'm just here long enough to see what's goin' on with Terry and Michael, I'm a little bit worried."

"Right now, Michael is better than he's ever been and we know about what's goin' on with Terry so is it that you don't believe what we're tellin' you?" He asked him as Irene handed Annette over to him.

"You know me man, I need to see before I believe." He said. "Missouri the show me state kind of thing, you know what I mean?" He said in a half joking manner.

"What is it that you're wantin' to see David, help me out." Douglas told him. "Didn't we talk about this on the phone a few days ago?"

"Talkin' about it and seein' it for myself is two different things my man and it's not just them that I wanted to see." He began. "I get this text message from Terry right after she got up here tellin' me that everything I told her about you wasn't true and that I needed to come and see how you've quote unquote "made" it up here."

"We're livin' one day at a time just like everybody else so don't be fooled by what you think you see."

"David are you gonna stay for dinner?' Irene asked him then.

"If you have enough for me to stay babe, I hear you have six mouths to feed."

"It's more than enough here, just let me know."

"Are you plannin' on tellin' me how you're doin' this man?" David asked him then. "It wasn't that long ago that you were down there in St. Louis doin' everything you were big enough to do and that's the last thing that I remember about you." "That's why I talked to Terry like I did, she needed to understand where I was comin' from."

"And it doesn't really matter what you said to her, we're talkin' about today."

"I am talkin' about today man, what're you doin' to make it like this?" He asked as his temper began to surface out of rage and jealousy towards him.

"Put her in the playpen down there honey, I'll let you know when this is ready." Irene told Douglas as she noticed him motion for David to follow him downstairs to his home office and "prayer closet."

"So is this where you keep all of your secrets man?" David asked him a few minutes later as he sat down in the office after Douglas closed the door behind him.

"I don't have any, but I do know that there is somethin' that's eatin' you alive when it comes to you and me." He told him as he sat down behind his desk.

"You have a light, I didn't wanna do this in front of your baby." He said as he got a cigarette from his pack in his shirt pocket.

"That's not happenin' in here, baby or not." He calmly told him.

"Since when dude, I can remember you goin' through two packs a day, is that part of your package too?"

"Tell me what my package means to you." Douglas said as he openly and boldly challenged him for an answer. "Let me have it because I know that it's there so this is the time to clear some major air."

"Are you sure about that?" He asked him. "How much time do you have?"

"As long as it takes because by the time you leave out of here, this whatever it is will be history."

"Man from the time you were a kid, it was all about you and what you wanted and to this day, I can't figure it out." David began after a moment. "I can remember even askin' mother what it was about you that made you so special to her and all she could tell me was that she felt guilty because you and Doris are only eleven months apart and you missed out on a lot because of that." He said, referring to their sister. "So I guess she called herself makin' things up to you and if you ask me, she went overboard with that, that was a lie."

"I've heard that from her before and I don't know how true it is but what does that have to do with now?" Douglas asked him. "If she went out of her way to try to make me feel better, I don't remember anything about it but what does that have to do with today?" He asked him again. "You're bringin' up stuff that went on thirty years ago or more so don't you think it's past time that you moved beyond that?"

"What I'm seein' now has to be because you're still dealin' drugs or you're doin' illegal stuff under the table because it just doesn't happen like this man unless you're pullin' some strings somewhere dog." He insisted. "You need to come clean with me and both of us will feel better."

"If you want to believe that, that's up to you, I don't have any control over that." Douglas said unphased as he got up, went over to the file cabinet in the corner and opened the top drawer. "Have you ever seen somebody die right in front of you David?"

"What's the matter, are you about to finally let me see the side of you that's not perfect?" "Did you take somebody out and you need to get it off your conscience or somethin?" He asked him with a tone of mockery in his voice.

"I don't think I've ever told you about this but it's because of what happened that day, that you're able to see me in the middle of all this stuff that you're so caught up in." He said, ignoring his comments as he handed him the newspaper article from eighteen years before, detailing the indelible scene of Phillip Mason's motorcycle accident. "I saw this man's head come off of his body; he lost control of his bike because we were sharin' a joint and the whole thing was over after he lost control and hit a telephone pole." Douglas continued. "We were high and on our way to a crack house to get more-

"Man-

"Hear me out David, I'm just gettin' started." He said, interrupting him. "It took that to knock some sense into my hard head and if it hadn't been for the mercy of God, I probably wouldn't be here talkin' to you." "It was because of that day that I almost put a forty-five to my head and would've blown my soul into Eternity but because of the grace and mercy of God, I'm still here." He emphasized again. "And my point to you is that all of this that you see and are so impressed with belongs to the Lord that saved me from myself and gave me another chance to get it right." He continued. "And don't get me wrong, I can't tell you how thankful I am that I've been able to put all of that behind me and start over but it all goes back to the goodness of God that I can't talk too much about David." "This is not a joke, I don't take it for granted and the next time that you feel like you can come in here and throw some weight around, think twice about it man."

"You never told me that all of this went on and this explains a lot." David said as he read the article.

"And I don't want you to get the impression that I'm on some kind of holier than thou trip because I'm not about that." Douglas told him. "And every opportunity that I get, I have to let people know how quick and easy it is to check out of here and if you're not ready to go, it's not a pretty picture."

"When did this happen?" He asked as he stared at the article.

"That was a little over eighteen years ago but I remember it like it was yesterday and I keep that as a reminder of how much a vapor life is." "That's why I don't get caught up with all of this stuff because number one, I'm not takin' any of it with me when I leave here and I have to concentrate on keepin' my soul ready to die or fly, whichever comes first."

"So you were about Michael's age when this happened." David said with a sober tone.

"I was twenty- two, he's almost twenty- four and before he got off into all of the stuff that I did, he got himself together and let the Lord save him so he's in a better place than he was just a couple of months ago."

"I'll see him when he gets here and I need to see Terry too before I head back."

"She gets off at ten and one of us will go pick her up; we're workin' on gettin' her a car but until that happens, she doesn't need to walkin' home that late."

"Man that's what she does, she's used to that and like I was tellin' Irene, don't be surprised when somethin' drastic happens to her because one of these times, it'll catch up with her." He said as he handed the newspaper article back to him.

"She's in God's hands, don't worry about her." Douglas told him in a matter of fact way.

"How can you not worry about her?" David asked him. "You of all people know what it's like out there and just because you have a little bit of faith, that's not the cure all for everything."

"I'll let you know how that goes." Douglas told him then as he refused to indulge in an argument with him. "Are you ready to come up here for dinner?" He asked him as he started towards the door after filing the newspaper back into the file cabinet.

"You're the boss man, how can I say no?" He said as he stood up. "I don't know how you did it but you're the boss."…

May 10, Sunday

"We're gonna come help you start packin' up boxes so you can go into labor, you look miserable woman." 'Nita told Donna Sunday afternoon after church at dinner.

"I've already started but I'll take all of the help I can get because this is gettin' serious." Donna said as she slowly sat down with a plate.

"And this is Michael's house now, it's official." Sheila said. "Me and Ruth are out of here in thirty days so he can start workin' on it and makin' it like he wants it."

"And Aunt Frances sold it to him for a dollar, how is he doin' all of this stuff so quick?" 'Nita said. "I'm jealous."

"We were talkin' about that this mornin' after Sunday School and he said that he had been really prayin' about findin' his own place because Terry's there now and it was startin' to get sort of crowded, he gave her his room so he's been crashin' on a air mattress." Sheila began. "Then Wednesday after they closed, James called him and asked him to come over here because they needed to talk to him about somethin' and he said he got scared."

"He thought he had done somethin' wrong and he was about to get it." Donna said.

"The next time I see him, I'm gonna have to work him over and tell him to stop bein' paranoid." 'Nita said.

"And he was tellin' me how much he's learnin' about what faith can do, he's still in shock over the whole thing." Sheila said.

"Where is he anyway?"

"Him and Janice are together somewhere, Sunday is their day to keep each other company." Sheila said as she poured more iced tea in her glass.

"Do you think they're a permanent thing?" Donna asked her.

"It's too soon to say that, she told me other day that they're prayin' about each other so they're not goin' there yet." I think she's afraid to really trust it yet because when you get kicked to the curb like she was, you get gun shy as Aunt Frances says."

"She needs to quit it, anybody can see that the Lord is all in that and I'm not even in there like everybody else around here." 'Nita said.

"I need to walk, go with me." Donna told her a moment later as she slowly got up from the table.

"If you don't go into labor tonight I'm gonna make you take some castor oil and make it happen woman." 'Nita told her as they started out the door.

"So you're sayin' that the only reason that you haven't gotten it up to now is because of other people that you know that are half steppin' as you say?" Donna asked her a few minutes later as they started walking around the block.

"Yeah pretty much and I just don't wanna be like that, you know what I mean?"

"I know what you mean but that's an excuse honey, you don't have any control over what other people do or don't do, you have to let the Lord save you because you're the only one that you have to give an answer for." She said as she slowed down with a contraction.

"I got part of it, I got baptized last year so I'm makin' some progress." 'Nita said as she waited on her to catch up.

"So is it mainly kids that you see at school that're actin' like they don't have anything?" Donna asked a moment later as she began to hold her back.

"And you know it." She said as she winced in pain. "We need to get back to the house, I'm not trustin' you."

"Hold up 'Nita, let me stop for a second." Donna said as she leaned against a nearby fence.

"Woman don't you have this baby out on this sidewalk, you're scarin' me, no kiddin.'"

"Do you have your phone with you?"

"I ran out of minutes, you didn't bring yours?"

She shook her head.' "I didn't think I'd need it, I left it on the table." She barely said as she braced with another pain after she felt her water break.

"Get her in here." Douglas said as he pulled up then after noticing her.

"Did the Lord send you down here or somethin'?" 'Nita asked him as she went over and took her arm.

"Douglas you're gonna have to do this, I am so sorry." She said apologetically a moment later as 'Nita opened the passenger side door.

"Quit lyin' Donna that is not funny."

"Stay right there, don't move." Douglas said as he got out and opened the back end door of the van.

"I'm not lyin' 'Nita, this is happenin' now." She said as she inched her way towards the back as he met her half way. "Douglas I am so sorry." She said again in tears.

"Don't worry about it, we'll talk about it later." He said trying to put her at ease. "See if you can get nine one one." He said as he gave 'Nita his phone.

"Anything I can do to help you?" A neighbor asked after seeing what was happening from her porch.

"If you have a bucket and a couple of towels that'll help." Douglas said as he helped her into the back. "This is gonna be over really quick, trust me." He told her attempting to reassure her.

"Why am I on hold?!" 'Nita said then in frustration. "This is crazy."

"End it and call it again." Douglas told her. "Donna this is it honey, one more push is gonna do it." He said as he knelt down on one knee after seeing the top of the baby's head.

"Why is this happenin' like this?" Donna said as she held herself up with her arms as she tried to stay calm.

"We don't know but it is what it is." Douglas said as they started to hear sirens.

"I got 'em honey you can put that down, come over here and help your friend have her baby." She told 'Nita as she stood back watching the birth.

"You got your girl Donna, hold on a second." Douglas told her a minute later as he wrapped her in one of the towels as she began to cry and breathe. "They're almost here so I'm gonna let them cut her loose." He added as he handed her over to Donna, still wrapped up. "Is Randy workin'?"

She nodded a little, still overcome by the ordeal but obviously relieved as the E.M.T.s arrived to take over.

"Are you the father sir?" Douglas was asked by one of the technicians as they strapped Donna and the baby onto a stretcher.

He shook his head while wiping his hands with one of the towels. "This is my sister-in-law and it's a long story so we'll just thank God and go on." He said.

"Good job sir and congratulations, this is a beautiful baby she's got here."

"You know that the Lord made you come down this street, how did that happen?" 'Nita asked him as she wiped her face.

"I was about to turn on mother's street and there was an accident that they were cleanin' up, and I couldn't get down there so I had to turn around and come this way." He said after a moment.

"But what would have happened if you didn't come down here Douglas, this is crazy." She said, still shaken.

"Like I said, just thank God because He knew all about this." "And the only reason I knew what to do was because I've been in the delivery room more than once with Irene so this is not the first time I've seen this happen, believe me." He told her as he walked her over to the van and opened the door so she could sit down and calm herself. "I need to go talk to Donna before they take off, give me a minute, I'll be right back.

"Did he say that he would meet me there at the hospital?" Donna asked him a minute later as they took her blood pressure before heading out.

"They're sendin' another driver to get him off his route but he'll be there." "And don't worry about the boys either, I'll have Irene call you later."

"You know, you look a little familiar to me." The neighbor said to Douglas as the ambulance left a minute later. "I'm Barbara Mason and I think I've seen you somewhere before." She added as she stared intently at him.

"Hey Douglas I need to walk back, I'll see you in a minute." 'Nita said as she got back out of the van.

"Are you okay now?' He asked her.

"Yeah, I just need to walk this off." She told him as she started walking back towards the house.

"Did you know my son Phil?" Barbara asked him as she began to remember the connection from years before.

"I did, I was right there with him before he had his accident." Douglas said as he began to clean his hands again with baby wipes from the van.

"You're not Douglas are you?" She asked him after a moment. "Didn't everybody used to call you junkyard?" She added as her eyes began to tear up.

He nodded in agreement. "That was me but that was a long time ago so you have a good memory." He told her as he noticed her emotions coming to the surface.

"Do you have a few minutes to talk to me?" She asked him with pleading in her voice. "I know that you just delivered that baby so I won't keep you long." She said apologetically.

"Sure I do, you look like you need to sit down." He said as he opened the door for her to sit in the front seat of the van.

"Did you say that you were with Phil when he had the accident?" She asked him half a minute later as he sat with her in the front seat.

"I was, we were on our way to a crack house on motorcycles and I'm sure you already knew that about him." Douglas began after a moment as he painfully and regretfully recalled the last moments of his friend's life.

"And I used to tell him all of the time to leave that stuff alone but he couldn't seem to get away from it." Barbara said in frustration. "He was all I had and it wasn't fair for him to leave me like that and we couldn't even have a funeral for him because he was so messed up."

"I saw it happen and it messed me up too and I was at the point where I was about to take myself out of here because of what I saw." He told her. "And every time the Lord gives me a chance to tell somebody how He got me out of that lifestyle that we were in, I have to talk about it." He added with emphasis.

"So you're tellin' me because you saw Phil die you gave all of that up just like that." She said to him with skepticism.

"That's exactly what I'm sayin', it shocked me into reality and I wasn't easy to affect like that but God knew what it would take to get my attention." He continued as he wiped his eyes with a handkerchief.

"And I see that it's still affectin' you after all of these years isn't it?" She asked him.

"I can still see it like it was yesterday but I won't let it stay in my head, the Lord has given me power over things like that that are destructive." He said. "God is about life and what we just saw happen is what I have to concentrate on and when I got up this mornin' I had no idea that I would have to do that but this whole thing was meant to be."

"I can't believe how calm and cool you were about it, have you had to do that before?"

"I've never had to do it before today but I have six kids and I've watched the doctors do what they do so it wasn't anything I haven't seen before, but I really didn't have much choice did I?" He asked her.

"I guess you're right about that, you said that was your wife's sister?"

"Yes ma'am but like I said, it's life and that's what God loves so it is what it is." He said.

"I guess that's a good way to look at it and I want to thank you for listenin' to me for a few minutes, it helped to talk about it." Barbara said then. "You don't live around here do you?"

"My mother -in-law lives one street over and I was on my way over there but I got sidetracked didn't I?" He said laughing a little.

"Yes you did and I'm proud of you for handlin' it like you did and if you're in the neighborhood again, feel free to stop by and talk to me any time." She said. "I'm sixty- five years old now and since I don't have Phillip anymore, you're the closest thing to him that I can have since you were the last person on earth to talk to him."

"I'll remember to do that because I'm over here pretty often and I'll be prayin' for you too." He told her as he started the ignition. "And now that I know where you are, we'll talk some more because there's a lot more that I need to tell you.".

"I thought she was lyin', you know how 'Nita is." Sheila said half an hour later after Michael and Janice came in from their dinner out.

"Wait a minute, go back to the beginnin' Sheila Scott." Michael told her as they sat down at the table. "I get this text from Irene sayin' that Douglas just delivered Donna's baby in the back of their van and I almost choked, no kiddin.'"

"We were sittin' in here eatin' dinner and Donna gets up from the table all of a sudden and tells'Nita to go walkin' with her." She began as she started to run dishwater. "She was havin' pains but she didn't really seem to be doin' that much to me."

"Sheila you're scarin' me." Janice said.

"Don't be scared, you'll probably be in labor for twelve hours because this is your first one." "Donna had three before today so that makes a lot of difference but anyway, 'Nita said they were talkin' about church stuff and she stopped in the middle of the sidewalk and started to hold on to a fence."

"Where is she now?"

"She walked back after it was all over and Douglas came back here and took her home, she was still sort of shook up and he looked like he had been shot."

"And he probably acted like it wasn't that big of a deal didn't he?" Michael asked her. "And how did he just happen to be there at the right time and place?"

"He had to come down that street over there because there was an accident that they were cleanin' up and he couldn't come down here." Sheila said shaking her head. "And you know that had to be God, it can't be anything else." "He was comin' over here to get a couple of plates for Irene and Chris because they're at Donna's house packin' and cleanin' up over there before they move out."

"And Randy's workin' today so he missed it all."

"Douglas said they were gettin' him off his route so he might be at the hospital by now."

"We have to go see her, I need to hear her side of it, that is just too crazy." Janice said.

"I'll take you if you wanna go now because I need to hear this too." Michael said. "And where's my best friend, is she here?"

"Her and James and Paul and all of the kids are out at the lot and they probably know by now what happened." Sheila said as she sat down with them. "So have you decided how you're gonna change stuff in here yet?"

"I was layin' awake the other night tryin' to decide what to do in here and I'm probably gonna have to get with James about some stuff." Michael said as his ringtone went off.

"That was quick." Sheila said after he hit the ignore button on his phone.

"I think I'm gonna have to get my number changed." He said, obviously annoyed.

"Uh oh, I smell a rat." Sheila told him.

"Does it live in St. Louis?" He asked her.

"Okay Michael, come clean, you're among your friends." Sheila told him as she sensed his displeasure. "And let your Holy Ghost work, it's okay." She assured him as she patted his hand.

"Believe me, I am and I know it's workin' because if this had happened a month ago, it would've been a whole different thing." He said, shaking his head.

"If what had happened Michael, don't be scared to talk, we have to keep this stuff real." Sheila told him.

"One of his old girlfriends has been sendin' him some X-rated selfies of herself to him." Janice spoke up then.

"Yeah you're right, you need to get your number changed." Sheila said then. "You need to stop that mess like yesterday."

"And if that's not bad enough, I think Terry's been tellin' her to do it." Michael said.

"What makes you think so?' Sheila asked him.

"This girl pretty much told me that she did so it's at the point now where I'm gonna have to sit my little sister down and help her out."

"So are they friends or somethin'?"

"They knew each other but I don't think they were friends like that but I know why she's doin' this and it won't work." He said decisively. "I keep tellin' her that it's a different thing with me now and she's doin' things to try to make me prove it."

"Then stop tryin' to tell her and just let her see it." Sheila said. "And if I were you, I don't think I'd say one word to her about it because then she might start to think that it's gettin' to you."

"It's like tryin' to fight your own battle huh?"

"Exactly and when you do that, God doesn't get the glory out of your victory and you are comin' out on top, you know that don't you?"

"I do now Sheila Scott." He said, amused.

"Hey I'm serious brother, you have to fight fire with fire and that kind of stuff is just a test that you're gonna pass." Sheila told him. "And you did delete it didn't you?"

"Is the grass green and the sky blue?" Michael asked. "You better know it and the first thing tomorrow when I get off from work, this number's gonna be history."

"Can't you put a block on it instead of havin' to go through the trouble of a new number?" Janice asked him.

"I'll find out tomorrow, I'm not lettin' this throw me off tonight." He said. "Do you still wanna go see your new niece?" He asked her.

"Yeah I do, let's go now before it gets too late.

"It was like I can't believe that this was happenin' to me, I didn't know that you could have a baby that quick." Donna remarked two hours later in her hospital room with Janice and Michael.

"Now you know." Michael said. "Have you talked to Douglas since you got here?"

"Not yet, I'm still tryin' to get over that part of it, that was not a joke." She said recalling the moments.

"Have you named her yet?" He asked as he cautiously approached the portable crib to get a close look at her.

"We decided on Sara and when Randy first saw her he just broke down, he's been wantin' a girl from the beginnin.'" Donna said as she noticed how fascinated he seemed to be with her. "You can hold her Michael, she won't break." They checked her out and she's okay."

"She looks like Randy too so you know he's gonna spoil her don't you?"

"I'll let him have his fun and the boys aren't gonna know how to act with a girl in the house."

"Chris told me that they have everything ready for you to move out Friday so that means we have to gone by Friday or Saturday." Janice said as she noticed how at ease he appeared to be as he gently and carefully picked her up out of the crib and sat down with her. To her, it was a small and seemingly insignificant illustration of how he could possibly be with her baby.

"Are you gonna tell her how she got here?" Michael asked her.

"When she gets old enough to understand I'll tell her that the Lord sent uncle Douglas down the street just in time or she might've been born out on the sidewalk, I'm not kiddin'." Donna said, shaking her head. "And I might've had to do it myself 'cause 'Nita was in worse shape than I was but it's over and we're done and it's all good."...

CHAPTER 4

MAY 12, TUESDAY

"How come you didn't tell me that you got your number changed Michael, what's up with that?" Terry asked him Tuesday night as they sat at the table in the basement kitchen after work.

"You don't have any idea why?" He asked her as he opened a can of pop. "When was the last time you talked to Kayla?" He said referring to his last girlfriend in St. Louis.

"She called me last week and wanted to know what happened to you." "She said she tried to call and text you but you wouldn't call her back." She lied as she attempted to cover herself.

"I hadn't heard from her since I left and then all of a sudden, I'm gettin' these dirty pictures of her on my phone so I had the number changed so it wouldn't happen again." Michael told her as he watched her reaction when she realized that her lie had been exposed.

"So I can't get your new number now huh?" She asked him after a moment.

"Did you tell her to do that or somethin'?" He calmly asked her as his spirit kept him from "blowing" up at her.

"I just wanted to see what you would do so now I know." She said, shrugging it off. "What's the big deal, it's not like it was anything new to you Michael, get real dude." "We used to talk all of the time so I know stuff about you that you probably don't want me to know." She added as she dipped her french fries in ketchup.

"So what did you think I was gonna do Terry?" He asked her, ignoring her last comment.

"What do you think, act like a man." She said irritably. "Did you let Janice see what you saw?" She said as she continued to taunt him, waiting for his negative reaction.

"Are you serious?" Michael asked her in amazement. "Why would I do that?"

"So she could see what she needs to be doin' if she wants to keep you." She said boldly. "She needs to know that you're not gonna keep this up too much longer because you're not the type."

"You really do have a major problem don't you?" He asked her then as he began to compassionately realize the serious nature of her problem.

She didn't answer him but shrugged again as if to convey to him her lack of concern about her issues. "I might but it's me and nothin' or nobody is gonna change me 'til I get ready." She said with a stubborn and rebellious spirit. "Do you still love me?"

"I don't think you realize how much I do because if I didn't, I wouldn't care about what happens to you." He told her.

"Are you gonna promise not to tell Douglas what happened?" She asked him.

"There's really no reason why he would have to know that, this is between you and me but you need to promise me that you won't ever try that again because it's not gonna work Terry." He told her.

"But how do you know, why is this such a big deal to you now when you used to live for it?"

"Terry if I tried to explain it to you, you wouldn't understand it so all that I can tell you is that until you see a ring on my finger, that's not happenin.'" He told her after a moment. "I'm not gonna try to get deep with you so for right now, that has to be good enough." He told her with an air of finality.

"So you think I'm not smart enough to understand where you think you're comin' from." She said to him.

"No that's not it ma'am, you're not anybody's dummy, but it wasn't that long ago that I learned the hard way that you just don't go there when you're livin' the way God meant for it to be." He said after a moment.

"How do you mean the hard way?"

"I had the nerve to try to make a move on Janice because that was what I was used to doin' but she let me know that that wasn't happenin.'" He began. "And I didn't understand what was goin' on with that either but things change and it is what it is."

"And she's pregnant with some other dude's baby and you're still actin' like that doesn't make any difference to you." She said. "I really don't know you anymore do I?"

"I'm still me and all of that but there's some things that I just don't do anymore and that stuff that you and Kayla thought up won't do anything but make me more determined to keep it right." He said. "Things are too crazy for me to try to make it without the help of God and I have to be ready to get out of here when the Lord comes." He added. "And that's the bottom line, that's what this is all about."

"So when is that supposed to happen?" She asked him with skeptism.

"That's what we don't know but I can't be wastin' my time out there messin' my life up just because I don't know." Michael said. "I mean my eyes came way open about myself when I got here and the bottom started to fall out of everything and that's how the Lord showed me how much help I needed." "I was a hot mess and it wasn't 'til I started talkin' to Irene's mother that I started to realize how real He is and what He'll do when you just give up and start to believe that He'll help you."

"Yeah you told me about her one other time and Irene told me about how her and Douglas got to be so tight too."

"Did you hear about what happened Sunday?"

"Irene told me that he delivered her sister's baby in the back of their van." She said, shaking her head. "That is crazy."

"It is but he really didn't have much choice."

"So after you move out this week-end am I still gonna get to see you Michael?" She asked him.

"I'm just movin' twenty minutes away and when you get your car, feel free to come by." He told her. "And I'll be in and out of here because it'll be a while before I can actually stay there all of the time."

"And Janice is not movin' in there with you huh?"

"Not happenin' so I guess you're startin' to get it huh?" He asked her. "She's movin' out there to the country with Chris and James this week-end too so it'll be a lot different but you can still call me if you need somethin' or if you wanna talk or whatever." He assured her. "And I'm gonna give you my new number and this goes nowhere else Terry, I'm not kiddin.'" He said as he wrote it on a napkin.

She nodded a little. "Are you gonna let me see your new place?"

"There really won't be much to see because I'm gonna be workin' there most of the time."

"And she sold it to you for a dollar?"

"She did and she's movin' out there too so she's leavin' all of the furniture except her bedroom stuff." Michael said. "It's almost too good to be true but when God does things, He does it right I'm findin' out."

"You really let Douglas rub off on you didn't you?" She asked him after a moment.

"Like how, what do you mean?"

"Before you moved up here, you would never say stuff like that and now just about everything you talk about has somethin' to do with God and all of that and it's makin' me sort of uncomfortable around you."

"That's because I wouldn't be where I am if it wasn't for the Lord and if that bothers you or whatever, I can't apologize for that."

"Even David said somethin' about how you are and he told me to be careful because if I let my guard down, I would end up over the top like you and Douglas." She said.

"Did you see him last week when he was here?"

"Yeah he stopped in the store on his way back to St. Louis and I talked to him for a few minutes on my break." She answered.

"If that's the way he sees it, I can't change his mind." Michael said. "And you have your own mind so you have to decide for yourself what you think."

67

She nodded again. "I'm goin' to bed and thanks again for givin' me your new number, I won't call you unless I have to."…

MAY 14 THURSDAY

"C'mon uncle Douglas, you know you have to hold her." Sheila told him after he came in the back door Thursday evening as she handed Sara over to him.

"Where's Donna?" He asked as he took the baby from her.

"We finally got her to go to sleep, she really hasn't gotten any rest since Sunday, there's too much goin' on." She said as they sat down at the breakfast nook. "Irene's not with you?"

"She's helpin' Chris get their last garage sale together for tomorrow, I just dropped her off and told her to call me when they're done." He said. "And what do you mean too much is goin' on Sheila Scott?"

"Donna's sort of bummed out because she thought she'd be bringin' her home from the hospital to their place, Janice is feelin' emotional because she won't be comin' back in here after today etc, etc." Sheila said.

"Is she here?"

She nodded. "She's in there helpin' aunt Frances get packed up and cleaned out and she just sort of lost it a few minutes ago."

"That's what pregnant women do, they lose it every now and then." Douglas said. "But I'll talk to her before I leave, how did she get here?"

"James dropped her off after they left work." She said. "But it's not just that, I'll let her tell you what's goin' on."

"There's my other son, I thought I heard you come in here." Frances said then as she came in the kitchen. "Sheila you have to get a picture of this honey." She told her as she stood next to him.

"I was just thinkin' that, this is just too special." She added as she picked up her phone. "Say cheese uncle Douglas."

"This is a good thing." Douglas said half an hour later as he came out to the porch where Janice was reading her Sunday school book.

"I didn't know you were here." She said as she looked up in surprise.

"I slipped in a few minutes ago." He said as he sat down on the bannister across from her. "Everything okay?" He asked her as he noticed her demeanor.

She nodded. "I'm okay, there's just so many changes goin' on and I'm probably too sentimental about things." She said.

"You mean this house and James and Chris old house?"

She nodded again. "And I know that Donna's gonna be in there and I can go any time but this house is where I got the Holy Ghost and it's just somethin' special about that." She added as she wiped her face.

"That was a pretty awesome night wasn't it?" Douglas asked her as he recalled her experience and the beginning of her spiritual journey.

"It was." "And I know that Aunt Frances is gonna be livin' with us in the new house but it's just not gonna be the same."

"But you'll be able to sit down and talk to her all the time now because she'll be right there, but I can see where you're comin' from, change is hard sometimes." He told her as he sensed something that she was holding back. "And what's Michael got to do with it?"

"I'm sort of afraid of the way that I'm startin' to feel about him." She blurted out. "And I should've known that you were gonna go there because you know me."

"A little bit but why are you afraid of it?" He asked her. "I have an idea why but I want you to tell me yourself because I might be wrong."

"I just keep thinkin' about how I let myself fall for Craig's talk and you see what happened to that." She began.

"Michael's not doin' that is he?"

"Not at all, he's just the opposite and that's what I really like about him, he actually does things instead of just talkin' about stuff."

"But you're not ready to really let yourself believe what you see." He concluded.

"If I do, I have this picture in my mind of goin' through what I did before and I can't do that anymore." She said after a moment. "And I'm gettin' a little bigger every week and I'm startin' to feel like that might make him change his mind about goin' any farther with this."

"So you have a shield up don't you?"

"I guess I do and I'm prayin' about it because I don't think that the Lord wants me to feel like this." Janice said, shaking her head a little.

"He doesn't and you're doin' the right thing by prayin' about that because He didn't give you the Holy Ghost so you could end up in the same shape that you were before."

"There's no way but I know if I don't let God help me, it could happen."

"And if I were you, I wouldn't worry about how you look, he noticed that the first time he saw you." Douglas told her as he noticed her spirit lift in response to his understanding words. "There would be somethin' wrong if you weren't changin' every week, that's progress." He added as it began to rain.

"But I'm just about half way, what am I gonna look like two or three months from now?"

"That's all a part of it and believe me, he knows it." "But you can't let things like that take your peace, you left that mentality behind because that doesn't do anything but make you miserable and that's not what the Lord wants for you."

"That's the thing, I don't feel like I deserve him and I'm sort of worried about him changin' his mind about things and that's stoppin' me from really lovin' him like I want to."

"Do you feel comfortable enough with him to tell him that?" Douglas asked her then.

"I'm gettin' there but I'm just not ready to put myself out there like that yet because he could change his mind and there I would be again." She said. "Marie called me the other day and she told me she saw Craig in the mall one day with some other girl that was about to pop so he wasn't doin' anything but usin' me up and that really made me glad that I don't have to deal with him anymore." "He is so history."

"It's called forgettin' those things that are behind you and movin' on as hard as that might be sometimes but don't let yourself be bound up with thoughts like that." "I could be wrong but I think he's serious so just keep doin' what you're doin' and you'll be okay."

"We have this thing that we can't talk to each other 'til we've talked to the Lord first and it's workin' out." Janice said as she noticed a woman walking erratically down the middle of the street, ignoring the heavy rainfall and the occasional traffic. "Is she okay?"

"What do you see?" Douglas asked as he turned around to take a look at what she was referring to.

"Is she drunk or somethin'?" Janice asked him.

"Stay right there hon, I think I know who this is." He said as he recognized her as Barbara Mason.

"Allright, what am I missin' out here?" Frances asked as she came out of the house then as she noticed Douglas headed towards her in the rain.

"She's walkin' out in the middle of the street and it looks like she's been drinkin' or somethin.'" Janice said as Frances sat down next to her with a glass of iced tea. "And can you tell me why he always gets mixed up in somebody's drama?" She asked her as they watched him approach her and lead her out of the street.

"Honey when you love people the Lord has a way of orderin' your steps to make sure that you're where you can make a difference." She told her.

"And I know that we have to help people when stuff happens but it's kind of scary, you know what I mean?" Janice asked her as they saw him open the door of the van and help her in.

"Are you afraid that somethin' might happen to him or somethin'?"

"It's just that everything is so crazy out here and things happen so quick." She said with a worried tone in her voice as he started back towards the porch.

"He knows how to take care of himself, don't let thoughts like that worry you." Frances told her. "Do you know her honey?" She asked him a moment later.

"She lives on forty third street over there where Donna had the baby the other night." He said. "She's Phillip Mason's mother."

"You are not serious." Frances said, surprised. "But I know that you are."

He nodded. "Is Sheila doin' anything right now?"

"Are you takin' her back home?"

"She's been drinkin' and she doesn't need to be out here." He said as he went back into the house to get dried off.

"What happened to you?" Sheila asked him a minute later as he came into the kitchen where she was cleaning up. "I got the kids in before they got wet, they're upstairs in my room watchin' Spongebob."

"If you have a few minutes I need for you to go for a ride with me around the corner." He told her. "I'll tell you about it later."

"Hold up a second, let me get my umbrella."

"We'll watch the kids, take your time and do what you have to do." Frances told him as he and Sheila started towards the van a minute later.

"Do you remember what happened out here Sunday afternoon?" Douglas asked Barbara five minutes later after he parked in front of her house.

She didn't say anything but stared intently at him, trying to recall what had happened.

"You were Phillip's friend." She said after suddenly remembering him.

He nodded a little. "We talked about that the other day."

"Did you know that today is his birthday?" She asked him as she began to cry uncontrollably. "This is not fair to me, he was all I had so why did God take him away from me?"

"Nobody knows the answer to that and I know how much it hurts because we were close and I saw him lose his life, I was there when it happened." Douglas told her with heartfelt compassion.

"Do you have any other relatives around here?" Sheila asked her then as she tried to empathize with her.

"He was all that I had." She said again with emphasis. "And the last thing he said to me that night was don't wait up for him and the next thing I know, the police were at the door to tell me what happened to my child." She said as she began to heave before Sheila quickly opened the sliding door and got out to help and prevent her from vomiting inside the van as it continued to rain.

"See if you can get her up on the porch Sheila, I'll be up there in a second." He told her a minute later after she had regurgitated on the street.

As Douglas sat there after listening to the few words that Barbara had just spoken, he became overwhelmed at the thought of what she was enduring. He began to recall the moment that he had distracted his friend with a shared joint, which had indirectly caused his fatal accident, still indelibly embedded in his consciousness after eighteen years. Then as he allowed the Lord to remind him of his grace and mercy towards him that had spared his life for a greater purpose, his recollection of past regrets abruptly turned into a spirit of rejoicing. The undeniable fact of the transforming power of the spirit of God was enough in itself to cause him to remember the powerful word of God that admonishes to forget those things which are behind and to reach for the things that are before.

"Does this happen to you every year?" Sheila asked her as they sat on her porch a few minutes later.

"Do you have any children honey?" She asked as she avoided her question.

"Not yet." Sheila said as she noticed Douglas get out of the van and come towards them.

"Then you probably wouldn't understand what it feels like to lose your child, especially when it didn't have to happen." She said with an air of anger in her voice.

"Are you feelin' any better?" Douglas asked her after a moment.

"Just a little and I guess that I owe you two an apology but this is not an easy thing." She continued. "And when I see you and how you've made it, it makes me really sick because he could've made me really proud of him but he left me." She told Douglas as she began to cry again.

"And you know what?" "You're makin' yourself feel worse by talkin' like that." He told her. "What happened eighteen years ago can't be changed and as hard as this is, you're gonna have to make your mind up to leave that behind you and try to keep it movin' sweetheart." He added as she took one of his hands and made eye contact with him. "We can always remember him because he was your son and he was like a brother to me but we can't bring him back."

"I know that but it's harder for me today because this was his birthday." She insisted as he and Sheila patiently let her talk to them. "I would always take him out to dinner but that can't happen anymore." She conceded. "Can't you understand how hard that is?" She asked him with pleading eyes.

"C'mon, is it okay if we go inside?" Douglas asked her as he gently helped her to stand up when he noticed her emotions begin to escalate. "Try to calm yourself down." He added as he motioned for Sheila to follow them.

"Do you see how handsome he was?" Barbara asked her as she sat down on her sofa and handed her a picture of him that was sitting on the end table a few minutes later. "He looked exactly like his father but he never wanted anything to do with him so it was up to me to do it all."

"Do you remember how old he was right here?" Sheila asked her as she watched for Douglas' reaction as he sat down in a nearby chair.

"He had that taken when he turned eighteen, just a few years before he died out there on the street and that's what's left of him." She said as she pointed to a small urn containing his ashes that sat next to a lamp. "I had to do that because we couldn't have a funeral for him."

"Is it helpin' you to talk about him like this?" Douglas asked her then as he sat there twirling his car keys around on the ring.

"It's helpin' because you're here to listen to me." "Would you have a shot with me before you go?" She asked him then after a moment.

He shook his head. "Don't do that anymore ma'am."

"I can remember when you and Phil would come in here and almost pass out you loved it so much." She told him.

"That was before I knew better and it was after he died that I got the message that I needed to get myself together because it could've been me." He said. "That was the Lord's way of givin' me a chance to come out of all of that and I really don't think I'd be here if things hadn't happened like they did." Douglas said as he took advantage of the opportunity to witness to her. "I hate the way he left here but it woke me up and rocked my world and like I just said, I'd probably be dead by now because of the way I let myself live out there."

"So you think that if Phillip hadn't died like he did, you wouldn't be alive today?" Barbara asked him.

"Probably not because I had a hard head and I wasn't payin' any attention to what my soul was missing." He said as he recalled his life on the edge. "I knew somethin' wasn't there and that's why I was always high or drunk because I was tryin' to satisfy that part of me that needed salvation and none of that was workin.'" "It never has and never will."

"Well whatever happened to you must've worked because you look like you really have it together." She told him. "Can I ask you two to pray for me before you go?"

"Absolutely, prayer is always in order." Douglas told her as Sheila followed his lead as he stood up and approached her with authority and faith in the name of Jesus. Together they began to thank God for the privilege that they had to boldly come to the throne of grace as they interceded for Barbara for her comfort and strength in her grief.

"I felt that, that means a lot to me." She told them a few minutes later as she took a handkerchief from Douglas as they started towards the door.

"I'll tell you what, I'll give you this and if you ever feel like you need to talk or if you need somethin,' give me a call." He told her as he handed her a business card from his wallet. "I told Irene that I saw you the other day so she knows what's goin' on."

"Is that your wife, do I know her?"

"I don't think you do but she knew Phillip, we would all do the clubs and parties and all of that crazy stuff together."

"Do you think she would mind if I gave you a hug for comin' to see about me?"

"No she wouldn't and maybe when we get some time, I'll bring her by here to see you." Douglas told her as she embraced him.

"And you too honey, you didn't tell me who you are." She said, turning to Sheila. "Are you one of Douglas' relatives or somethin'?"

"He's my cousin-in-law or somethin' like that." She said. "Irene is my first cousin." She said as Barbara hugged her.

"You're lucky to have him, he's wonderful person." She said as she wiped her face again with the handkerchief. "When I talk to Phillip tonight, I'll let him know that you stopped by."

"Did you hear the last thing that she said right before we left?" Sheila asked as she and Douglas sat in the van in the driveway five minutes later after coming back.

"I did and sometimes when you've been drinkin', you say things that don't make much sense." He said as he thought about his own experience.

"But I still don't understand how you hooked up with her in the first place." She said. "Back up some."

"I was sitttin' on the porch talkin' to Janice and she happened to see her walkin' out in the middle of the street in the rain." He began. "I think she could tell by the way she was walkin' that somethin' wasn't right so I went out there and got her in here to keep her from gettin' hit by a car or somethin.'"

"And you said you met her Sunday when you were over there playin' Dr. Johnson huh?"

"She had some towels and a bucket and that's how we hooked up and I'm seein' now that that whole thing was meant to be." He told her. "But I'm seein' more and more that we need to stay in a place where we're able to help people out here because there's a lot of stuff goin'on."

"Yeah I know it is, and when I hear about the issues that some of the people on my job are goin' through, it just makes me so thankful that I got the Holy Ghost when I did because I know myself." Sheila said. "I would've been out there caught up in some mess that I couldn't get myself out of."

"And don't ever lose that because it's too easy to sit back and tell yourself that you have what it takes to make it, and then forget about where God brought you from." He said. "That's kind of a dangerous place to be because you don't want any reminders from the Lord to keep you in line."

"Has that ever happened to you?"

"In over eighteen years, probably so and even when we were talkin' to her today, all of that stuff tried to come back." "I had to remind myself that there had to be a reason why I wasn't the one to leave here like he did and it keeps you humble and thankful, believe me when I tell you." He concluded.

"How's Terry doin', I still haven't had the chance to meet her."

"Just keep her in your prayers because after that last incident between her and Michael, that's what it's gonna take."

"You heard about that huh?"

"I did but she's just testin' him to see if he's really what he's claimin' to be and that's not always easy and before it's over with, he'll have a testimony." He said as he got a text message from Irene.

"I'll go up and get the kids, you probably need to sit here and let God help you, it's been a long night."...

CHAPTER 5

MAY 16, SATURDAY

"C'mon James, you know you need to cry don't you?" 'Nita asked him Saturday morning around five-thirty as she, Chris and Janice stood around in the kitchen as they waited on their movers to arrive.

"It's not like I won't be comin' back in here 'Nita Scott, it's all good ma'am." He said as Michael came in the back door with a box of doughnuts.

"Now we're talkin', where's the orange juice?" She asked him.

"Good mornin' to you too, do you know how much I'm gonna miss comin' in here where all of the fun is?" He asked as he immediatedly approached Janice.

"You know good and well that you're gonna be out there every other day because you can't stay away from the love of your life." 'Nita said as she opened the doughnut box.

"What time is the truck comin'?"

"They said six o'clock so we're just here killin' a little time." James said as he reached into his shirt pocket for the cashier's check.

"Did you get a chance to get all of the keys made?" Chris asked him as she opened all of the cabinets to make sure they were all emptied out.

"I did that last night baby cakes but I saved this for today." He said as he handed her the envelope.

"What's this, more paper work?" She asked him as she took it and started to look inside.

"Watch this." Michael told Janice as Chris looked at the check in bewilderment.

"What's this for?" She asked him, still puzzled.

"That's up to you mommy, you're in control of every dime of that." James told her.

"But where did this come from James, I'm not gettin' this." She said as she stared at the check and began to quietly cry.

"I just love them, they are openin' my eyes to a lot of things." Michael said then after James put his arm around her and lead her out.

"How much is it Michael?" 'Nita asked him. "And I know he told you so don't play dumb."

"I'll let her tell you, you're not gettin' me in trouble 'Nita Scott." Michael said as he took one of the chairs down from the table for Janice to sit down.

"You don't get in trouble, you're just bein' difficult."

"I told him I wouldn't say anything so I won't, case closed ma'am."

"So what's the plan, when are you movin' into your house over there?" "I know you can't wait so don't try to be cool about it because I know better."

"Probably one day next week, I have to make sure that everything she wants out of there is where she wants it." Michael said. "That's my best friend so I have to make sure she's taken care of first."

"Do you remember the day Jane's mother called me so she could meet me out at the lot?" James asked as he and Chris sat down on their stripped down bed a minute later.

"Is this where this came from?" She asked him. "I don't feel right takin' all of this, I need to talk to Jane."

"That's up to you honey, she gave that to me for workin' on their house but she said some stuff that day that made me not want it from her so it's yours." He told her.

"What did she say, it couldn't have been that bad James." Chris said.

"She's livin' in the past somewhere and when she started talkin' about havin' housekeepers and servants and all of that stuff, I almost lost it and let her have it but I had to let God help me."

"Does Jane know about this?"

"I haven't said anything to her but her mother might've but that's besides the point." "I'm thankful to the Lord for how all of this worked out but she pushed the wrong button that time." He said as he remembered the conversation. "Then when I told her that I was married to Paul's sister, it was like I had punched her in the gut, she was shocked and embarrassed and at the time, it just didn't matter, she took me there." He confessed.

"But if I'm not lettin' it get to me you can't let it bother you like it is because I'm over it honey, we have more important stuff to deal with."

"Have you taken that test yet?" He asked her after a moment, referring to her pregnancy test.

"Yeah I did and it was positive so it's a good thing that we decided on six bedrooms instead of four." She said as they heard the truck pull up into the driveway.

"And I love you too, let's do this."

"This feels so different but I think I might like this out here." Janice remarked around eight-thirty that night as she and Michael sat in his car in the driveway at the new house.

"It's somethin' about it that makes you want to sit and think and if I were them, the only reason I would drive into town would be for work and church."

"Did James tell you about Chris?"

"Yeah he said they weren't surprised but this is it and they're really glad that Aunt Frances is in here with them because she's not gonna feel like doin' that much right now."

"She told me that she's gonna be goin' back and forth between here and Jane and Paul's house over there so she's gonna be really busy."

"But that's a good thing, busy keeps you young and the longer she's around here the better off everybody'll be."

"So how much longer will it be before their house is ready?"

"We have all of the rooms painted and the bathrooms and kitchen stuff is comin' next week so it might be another two or three weeks before it's ready." He told her. "Have you walked around in there yet?"

"I looked in one of the windows a couple of weeks ago but I haven't been in there yet."

"Do you feel like walkin' over there?" "It's just about five hundred steps from here to there and Chris told me to keep you active." He said as he started to get out of the car.

"I need to ask you about somethin' that's really been botherin' me Michael." Janice said a minute later as they slowly began walking east towards Paul and Jane's house.

"I could tell, let me have it hon."

"How could you tell?"

"Because in the little time that I've known you, I can pretty much figure out when you're not yourself." He said. "Have I done or said anything that's got you sort of uptight?"

She shook her head as she attempted to express herself in a way that he would understand without embarassing herself.

"I think I'm startin' to love you Michael and I'm sort of scared to let myself go there with you because of the baby." She managed to say.

"So you're sayin' that you're afraid that I'll just all of a sudden one day decide that I don't want anything to do with you because you're carryin' somebody else's baby." He said after a moment.

She nodded a little before she spoke again. "And I know that we talked about this before but I'm startin' to get really worried about the way I'm startin' to look."

"But if you weren't changin', there would be somethin' wrong wouldn't it?"

"Douglas said it was progress but when I think about what it'll be like three or four months from now, I'm not likin' it." She admitted.

"Would you feel like that if she was ours together?"

"Probably not and I'm always thinkin' that you're gonna decide that we shouldn't go any farther with this." She said. "And then it'll be the same thing all over again with another guy and I hate feelin' like that."

"Then since you feel that way, I need to know what it is that I can do to keep you from feelin' so insecure because I don't want you to go through that again either."

"But it's not you, it's me that has this thing about not bein' able to trust men because of the ones that have kind of messed me over, you know what I mean?" She asked him. "And I'm prayin' every day for the Lord to help me because that's what it's gonna take."

"Has Aunt Frances ever told you about that scripture that says to forget those things that are behind and to go for what's ahead of you?" He asked her as he paraphrased the verse in his own words.

"She probably has and I really do need to start doin' that don't I?"

"I don't know about anybody else but just that one verse has gotten me over some stuff, because every now and then, somethin' will come up or somebody might say somethin' that'll bring things back to me that're just bad reminders."

"Irene told me one time that Douglas goes through that sometimes but he always keeps it movin'."

"And if it wasn't for him and James, I wouldn't be learnin' how to love and treat a woman right because we didn't really have anybody that would take the time to explain the way things are supposed to be."

"But your father was around wasn't he?" Janice asked him as they approached the house.

"He was there but he didn't really take any time with us and I think that might be some of Terry's problem."

"When am I gonna get to meet her?"

"I'm not sure that that would be a good idea right now, she has a problem with me because of us so I'm not givin' her the chance to start anything with you." Michael said as he opened the front door.

"This is huge, they are gonna be so excited to have all of this space." Janice said a few minutes later as she walked behind him room to room as he made sure there was nothing for her to fall over.

"And one of the best things about this is that Paul didn't have to pay anybody to design this, James really knows what he's doin'." He said as his ringtone sounded. "Hey Douglas what's up?"

"Where are you?" He asked.

"I'm out here at the lot with Janice." "What's goin' on?" He asked him as he detected a difference in his voice.

"How soon can you get to the hospital, Terry's here in pretty bad shape and you need to see this to believe it."

"We have her sedated because she was hysterical when she got here and from what we can tell from the police report, she was at a party and was gang raped." "She's lucky to be alive." The E.R. doctor spoke to Michael and Douglas an hour later. "We did an M.R.I. and she has a mild concussion but that's the less serious side of it because whoever was involved in this almost killed her."

"How many are we talkin' about?" Douglas asked him.

"From what we got from the police, they have five in custody and she knew two of the guys so it's not clear at this point what happened." The doctor continued. "If you want to go back to see her you can, but as I said, we have her sedated and she won't know that you're there."

A few minutes later as they approached her room, Michael immediately turned back around and left after taking a quick glimpse at Terry. After seeing her swollen unrecognizable face along with several bruises and lacerations all over her body, it was too much for him to see as he slowly walked down the hallway and began to silently pray through his tears.

"Michael." Douglas said half a minute later after catching up with him. "We can't run away from this because that's how you get defeated." He told him as he gently escorted him back into the room. "We have the Lord to thank for not allowin' the devil to take her out of here and we have to deal with this headon." He added as Michael stood over her shaking his head.

"Douglas we tried to tell her." He managed to say.

"I know we did but sometimes it takes more than talk and both of us know that God has a way of gettin' your attention and it's nothin' but His mercy that she's still here." "She's in bad shape right now but she's comin' out of this." He spoke with faith and authority.

"Did you call St. Louis?"

"I talked to Doris, she's flyin' up here so one of us is gonna have to meet her at the airport around eleven-thirty.

"Terry can you hear me honey?" Doris asked her two hours later in the I.C.U. with Douglas. "Tell me if you know where you are." She added as she started to take her pulse.

"She may not wake up for another hour or two Doris, maybe we need to just sit it out." Douglas told her as he stood up from a chair.

"I'm just concerned about that concussion because sometimes when that happens, your memory goes for a minute." She said as they started out of the room together. "And I've seen a lot of things come into the E.R. but nothin' quite this bad."

"Like I told Michael, she'll come out of this but that's no guarantee that she'll cut this stuff out."

"But she's been at it since she was thirteen or fourteen years old Douglas, she's sick." She concluded. "I don't know whether it's a physical or an emotional thing but somethin' has got to give or she might not make it next time." She added as they sat down in the waiting area.

"It might be a combination of both but I do know that this isn't too hard for God and that's what it'll take if she wants the help."

"Yeah I talked to David when he got back and he told me about how well you're doin' and it must be because of your faith and all of that good stuff." She commented. "You're lookin' really handsome and prosperous and if you weren't my brother, I might go after you."

"We won't go there, this is not about me." He said.

"I know it's not but you and Michael may have saved her from a lot worse by bringin' her up here like you did." She told him. "Every other night I see these girls come in the E.R. either shot or stabbed by some guy that picked 'em up off the street and most of 'em think that it wasn't gonna happen to them but they find out really quick how dangerous it is out there."

"Michael was shook up when he took a look at her but he has to know that this may be for her good in the long run."

"Have you been able to get her to go to church with you and Irene?"

"That's not on her radar and until she sees her need for help from God, she can go to church everyday of the week and it's not gonna affect her." Douglas said. "You have to come to yourself and see how helpless and undone you are before that does you any good."

"So what happened with Michael all of a sudden?" Doris asked him. "Terry would send me text messages tellin' me that she didn't know him anymore and she was feelin' like she couldn't talk to him like she used to."

"He was goin' through this thing where he couldn't find a job and one thing sort of led to another and one day Irene's mother sat him down and gave him some truth and the rest is history, I'll let him tell you about it."

"I can't wait to hear about that one because he was a hot mess too but in a different way."

"But everybody has a story and no two are alike but the bottom line is he got his help and I don't think you could pay him to go back to where he came from."

"So he's workin' the third shift like I usually have to do at the hospital."

"He's a dock supervisor at a wholesale warehouse and he started to call off because of this but he hasn't been on that job long enough to start that, I told him we would keep him posted." Douglas said as a nurse approached them.

Hi, I'm Megan and I'm taking care of your sister tonight and I thought you'd like an update." She said as she sat down next to Doris. "And I hear you're also an R.N. so you probably know what's going on but we need to communicate with you about her just the same." She said as she read over Terry's chart.

"Is she tryin' to wake up?" Doris asked her.

"When I checked on her she was showing some signs of trying to speak and that's a good thing but she's not out of the woods yet." She answered. "Her vitals are stabilized but we need to watch her for a full twenty-four hours just to make sure that she doesn't lapse into a coma because she does have a head injury."

"Do they have any idea how that happened?" Douglas asked her.

"From what they saw on the M.R.I. it was a blunt force trauma injury and we don't know if she fell or if she was hit with something but she does have a mild concussion and she may or may not remember what happened." She concluded. "But you're free to go back in there with her if you like and if you have any questions or concerns, I'll be at the nurse's station right outside the I.C.U."

"Okay Megan, thank you hon." Doris said as she and Douglas stood up. "I'll meet you in there, I need to talk to her doctor." She told him as she headed towards the restroom down the hallway.

A minute later as he walked into her room, he found her lying there with her eyes barely open, staring blankly towards the wall.

"Terry?" He asked as he cautiously approached her bed.

At the sound of his voice, she reacted by turning slowly and deliberately towards his direction, and then as she held her arms out to him, she unashamedly allowed herself to literally cry on his shoulder like a small child. As he sensed her feelings of anxiety, he began to quietly and instinctively enter into intercessory prayer mode which instantly calmed her as she reluctantly let him go and allowed him to help her lie back down a minute later.

"How come they wouldn't stop, they were all over me and they wouldn't stop." She wailed then through uncontrollable tears.

"Terry listen to me sweetheart." Douglas told her as he took one of her hands.

She managed to nod a little then.

"It's not going to do you any good to keep talkin' about what happened but if you can, start to thank God for watchin' over you because it could've been a lot different." He told her. "Whoever they were, they were arrested but that's not for you to worry about right now." He said as Doris came in.

"I'll try." She said as she winced in pain. Then as she looked up and saw Doris coming towards her an overwhelming feeling of comfort came over her as she began to realize that she had support coming from her family despite the gravity of her present situation.

"I'll be out here, take your time." Douglas told her as he left to give them their privacy.

As he walked back towards the waiting area, he was met by one of Terry's co-workers headed towards her room.

"Hey man, you're her brother aren't you?" He asked after turning back around after passing him. "Don't you pick Terry up from work sometimes?" He asked him, obviously shaken by what had happened. "I've seen you before."

Without saying a word, he took his arm and escorted him to the waiting area to talk to him.

"Man it wasn't supposed to be like this, is she gonna make it?" He asked him as his voice began to quiver.

"She will but that doesn't have anything to do with why it happened."

"We just decided to go to this party that a couple of my friends were havin' after work and we were just hangin' out, no big deal."

"I don't think you told me your name." Douglas said then.

"I'm Anthony and I work with Terry at the store a couple of days a week and we were just hangin' out." He said, repeating himself. "Then I went outside for a few minutes because they were startin' to smoke and get high in the house and I wanted to go out for some air, you know what I mean?"

"She didn't go out with you?"

"I had to leave for a few minutes to go pick my mother up from her job, I was comin' right back so I didn't even tell her I was goin'." He continued. "And when I got back to the house man, I couldn't find her nowhere and somebody told me they saw her go down in the basement with some guy she had been talkin' to but I didn't think that was a big deal, there was a lot of people there, I just thought the party was movin' down there 'cause it was startin' to get crowded upstairs." He finished as he fought to keep his composure. "Man I should've known, I went down there to see what was goin' on and I heard some stuff goin' down in this room with the door locked and nobody was doin' anything about it, they knew what was happenin' in there." He said through his frustrated tears.

"Is that when you called the police?" Douglas asked him as he passed him a box of tissue.

"I called 'em 'cause I could hear her cryin' and tellin' 'em to stop whatever they were doin' to her and it got worse, they were actin' like they were crazy man." "They were all over her like a bunch of animals or somethin'."

"When you're high or drunk, you don't really know what's goin' on and I'm not defendin' these guys whoever they are but that stuff messes with your mind."

"It was five of 'em in there with her and they almost killed your sister man." He said as he stood back up and nervously started pacing back and forth. "Is she gonna make it man, can I go in there to see her?"

"Her sister is in there right now and you probably need to wait until tomorrow before you try to talk to her but I can tell her that you were here."

"Man how come stuff like this happens when you're tryin' to do the right thing?"

"How do you mean?" Douglas asked him. "That works both ways, things happen when you're doin' the right thing and when you're not so that's just life but this could've been avoided."

"I tried to tell her over and over again to slow it down 'cause these niggas out here are bad news and now she knows it." He said as he started to become angry because of the whole incident.

"If it matters to you, I don't think she has a lot of control when it comes to this and I'm dead serious when I say that."

"Are you for real man?" Anthony asked, shocked at his response.

"I don't think she does and she may try to give you the impression that this is what she loves to do and all of that to cover her sickness up and that's what it is."

"Like when you get addicted to stuff like drugs and alcohol and all that crap?"

"Now you're gettin' it and I know what that's like and it's not a joke when you can't help yourself and I'm thinkin' that's her problem." Douglas told him. "I'm not defendin' her or anything like that but that's probably what's goin' on and until she gets to the point where she wants help, she may not be able to stop."

"So you're tellin' me that even after this happened, she still might go right back to it?" He asked him. "That's crazy man and you're her brother, can't you do somethin' to help her?"

"I'm doin' everything that I possibly can but this thing with her is somethin' that the power of God will have to heal and she has to want the help, otherwise she'll end up in the same stuff until it takes her out, one way or another." "I know that's a hard thing for us to deal with but it's the truth and I know first hand what it's like to be helpless like she is."

"Do you think that God cares about what happens to her like you and me do?"

"I know He does because if it wasn't for the Lord keepin' her from checkin' out of here tonight, we'd be plannin' her funeral and I don't say that just to be puttin' it out there either." He concluded.

"But how do you know that?" Anthony asked as he kept trying to make sense of what was going on.

"Because I know that God answers prayer when you believe Him and the way that her brother and me have been prayin' for her protection ever since she got here, I don't know what else it could be." He told him. "And if you don't remember anything else that I've said to you tonight, I think you need to know that you may have been the one that the Lord used to spare her young man."

"Because she's my friend man, she's like a sister to me and this hurts." He insisted.

"But doesn't it help to know that she's gonna be allright?" Douglas asked him as he felt his sincerity. "It'll take a little time but this'll be okay." He assured him.

He nodded as he slowly stood up and started back towards the emergency entrance. "Can you tell her that I was here?" He asked as he stopped and turned back around.

"I will and by this time tomorrow, she might be able to see you so we'll just take it one day at a time.".

MAY 17, SUNDAY

"I almost didn't recognize you honey, you don't look like you did the last time I saw you." Doris remarked as she and Michael embraced Sunday evening around five-thirty after he and Irene stepped off the elevator at the hospital.

"That's good to know, you don't look too bad yourself."

"And somebody's been takin' good care of you too Mrs. Johnson." She said as he hugged Irene.

"If you say so but it's not about us right now." She said as they sat down. "And Douglas told me that they got you a room up here so you wouldn't have to leave." "Have you had any sleep?"

"I laid down for a couple of hours after Douglas left and that was probably around three but I'm used to bein' up all night so it wasn't a big deal."

"He got home around four and crashed for a minute before he went to church to teach his Sunday school class then I told him to go back home and go back to bed." Irene said. "And the kids are out too, we took 'em to Adventureland yesterday so they're all out to lunch."

"So how is she?" Michael asked her.

"They gave her a strong sleep aid this mornin' around six and I've been checkin' on her every couple of hours just to make sure that she's not unconscious because of the concussion."

"Did she get a chance to talk to you before she went to sleep?"

"She tried to tell me about all of the stuff that went on but I had to stop her because it was just makin' things worse for her." Doris said, shaking her head a little. "And her friend that called the police talked to Douglas last night before he left and he was really shook up too."

"Is it okay for us to go in there now?"

"I don't know why not, she might be still sleep in there but you can try to talk to her." She said as they got up and slowly walked towards her room.

Two minutes later as Irene and Michael walked in, they found her sitting on the edge of the bed quietly but distinctly allowing the Lord to speak through her in an unknown language as unmistakable evidence that His spirit had taken up residence in her being. They were both speechless at what they were witnessing as once more God was proving Himself to be faithful to His promises.

"Call Douglas so he can hear this." Irene told Michael as she "lost" it in response to the presence of God in the room with them as they watched in amazement the sweet calmness Terry's demeanor as she continued to submit to what was happening to her.

"Hey Douglas, are you up?" Michael asked him a minute later, his voice trembling with emotion as he stood watching and listening to Terry fluently "talk" in another tongue.

"Don't give me any bad news, are you at the hospital?" He asked him as he noted the difference in his voice.

"Yeah I am , hold on a second." Michael managed to say as he put his phone on speaker for him to hear the "joy unspeakable" that was transpiring.

"Can you believe this?" Irene asked him through her tears after Douglas hung up two minutes later without saying a word, obviously too overcome to speak.

"Everything allright in here?" Doris asked then as she came in from the hallway.

"Neither could say anything as she stood there next to Michael transfixed by what she was observing.

"Is she okay?" She asked Michael, not understanding the magnitude of what she was seeing and hearing.

"We'll be back." Michael told Irene as he put his arm around her neck and walked out of the room with her.

She nodded as she continued to sit next to Terry on the side of the bed, patiently waiting on the Lord to complete what He does best; the baptism of His spirit upon another believer. It was an illustration of the outpouring of His unmatchable power that He promised to repentant and believing hearts, despite the outward appearance of what is seen by human eyes.

"The last time I checked on her, it looked like she was gonna be out for a while and that was probably about three or four 'o clock."

Doris remarked with Michael as they stood out in the hallway a few minutes later.

"It's okay, it's all good, believe me." Michael told her as he noticed her confusion from what she had just seen.

"She was talkin' but I couldn't understand anything that she was sayin.'" She said in bewilderment. "Do you know what she was talkin' about in there?"

"I have no idea but that's the Lord talkin' out of her and believe it or not, she's got her help now."

"Is that the speakin' in tongues thing that I've heard about?" She asked him suddenly. "Is that what she's doin'?"

"You got it and I can't wait to talk to her to see how this happened because before last night, this was the last thing on her mind."

"You know that sayin' about God workin' in mysterious ways?" Doris asked him with a nervous laugh.

"I sure do and that's why I can't wait to hear what she says." Michael said as his ringtone went off. "And this is Douglas, give me a minute."

"What's goin' on?"

"Man she's in another world so it might be a while before she comes back down to earth, I'm serious." Michael told him. "And we don't know how long she's been speakin' like she has but this is unreal."

"It's more real than you know but I called Sheila and her and Ruth came to stay with the kids and I'll be there in a few minutes."

"Doris went down to the cafeteria, I think this is makin' her a little uncomfortable." Michael said fifteen minutes later as he and Douglas walked towards Terry's room where she was still sitting on the side of her bed with Irene as she continued to "speak" as God clearly gave the utterance through her. They watched her as the countenance on her face suddenly changed as she began to come to herself and realize what was happening to her. She then quickly "jumped" up as best she could and began slowly pacing back and forth in the room as she felt the quickening power of God's spirit for the first time within her.

As Michael got up to close the door, he noticed Doris standing in the doorway observing what was going on and then motioned for her to join them as they continued to witness Terry's second birth experience.

"God gave it to me, God gave it to me." She finally spoke on her own then as she freely and openly wept without embarrassment. Then as she looked around and discovered Michael on one side of her, she nearly stumbled towards him before they embraced and cried openly together.

"He gave it to you and don't you let it go for anything baby." Douglas told her as she cried on him out of relief and joy.

"I'm so sorry, I am so sorry." She managed to say as a myriad of emotions began to flood over her as she thought back over the wilderness that she had just been delivered from.

"We're just tryin' to hear it from you about how this happened if you can remember the details." Michael said an hour later as they waited on her discharge papers. "This is unbelievable."

"After I got through talkin' to Doris last night, I started to think about what you said to me before you left." She told Douglas after a moment as she tried to recall her last twelve hours. "You told me to thank God for watchin' over me because they almost killed me." She said as she stared at the bruises left as reminders of her ordeal. "And that's what I did, I just started to talk to Him like He was in here with me."

"Did you know any of 'em?" Michael asked her.

She shook her head. "They were just some guys that were at this party and I had been talkin' to one of 'em and we ended up goin' back to this room in the basement-

"Terry you don't have to back through all of that unless it helps you to get it out but we're just tryin' to get an understandin' of how all of this came together for you like it did." Douglas told her. "I don't think you realize what a story you have and how many other people you might be able to help because of this." He added as she began to feel the power of her newly given spirit start to overtake her again.

She nodded as she attempted to describe to them her visitation with the Lord before He poured out of His spirit into her. "And then that was when I started to think about how sorry I was for the way I've been actin' and talkin' and all of that stuff that I was doin'." She lamented as she tried to still herself. "I couldn't help myself and I wasn't tryin' to hurt anybody but I couldn't help myself." She repeated as Douglas, Michael and Irene patiently allowed her to finish such a testimony of the mercy and grace of Almighty God.

"Keep goin' honey, this is better than I thought it would be." Douglas remarked as he wiped his eyes with a handkerchief.

"I just kept tellin' God thank-you and then I started sayin' these words that I wasn't understandin' and I couldn't stop my mouth from movin'." She said as she attempted to describe her experience. "And then when I started to remember what you told me Michael about what happened to you, I just gave it up." She concluded as he could only shake his head at the thought of his testimony that had made a difference to her.

"So how much do you understand about what just happened to you?" Douglas asked her.

"I remember what you told me right after I moved up here from St. Louis about how I needed the help and the power of God to help me with my problem." She said after thinking a moment. "Do you remember the first time you picked me up from work that night we sat in the parkin' lot and talked for a few minutes?" She asked him as she got a tissue from a nearby box.

"I do and it wasn't easy to talk to you like I did but I had to tell you what the Lord gave me for you so I didn't really have a choice."

"And I was actin' like I didn't care what you were sayin' but you let me know that if I wanted the help I could get it."

"And believe me, you got it and whatever you do, never let anybody or anything make you go back because this is the gift the Lord promised us and this is what will keep you out of trouble if you allow it to."

"Don't worry, I think I learned my lesson and Michael I might not have believed a lot of what I was hearin' if it wasn't for what I saw from you." "You just don't know." She added as she let herself go once more as she again thought back to the bondage that she had been living in and the deliverance through her gift of the Holy Ghost, now abiding in her being.

"Are you ready to go get the rest of it?" Michael asked her as Doris came in with her discharge instructions.

"You got the spirit but you have to do the water part too." Irene told her.

"I get to get baptized too?" She said after processing what she had just said.

"Can you stand it?" Douglas asked her as he began to noticed the almost child like attitude that she had in contrast to her previous behaviour.

"How long do I have to wait?"

"You don't, this is the kind of thing that doesn't have to wait so as soon as we can check you out of here, we can get it done."

"Terry they just need your signature on this form and this is a script for Vicodin if you want it." Doris said as she handed it to her.

"I think I'll be okay without it, I'm just ready to leave here so I can start all over again." She said as she slowly got up out of the chair she was sitting in.

"And now my dearly beloved, for the confession of your faith, and for the confidence that you have in the Blessed Word of God, concerning the Death, Burial and Resurrection of Jesus Christ, I now baptize you in the name of Jesus, for the remission of your sins and you shall receive the gift of the Holy Ghost." The minister spoke over Terry an hour later as others tried to keep her still until the words were completed as she nearly lost her balance standing in the water in anticipation of the cleansing power of the shed blood of Jesus on Calvary's cross that erases and forgives sin completely and unconditionally.

As she came up out of the watery grave where transgressions are forever buried through the powerful name of Jesus, she repeatedly" jumped for joy" at the reaction of her soul for burdens of her heart "rolled away". It was the perfect illustration of the rewards of obedience to the Word of God, though not always understood but believed, which brought the result of salvation by child like faith. The effectual fervent prayers of the righteous had availed much by eliminating the device of the enemy intended to kill and destroy but because of the rich mercy and grace of God, death, hell and the grave were once more defeated...

CHAPTER 6

MONDAY, MAY 18

"I can't believe she sold this to you for a dollar, what did you do to deserve that?" Doris asked Michael as they walked through his house before going to the airport Monday afternoon.

"I didn't do anything and I'm callin' her my new best friend now but it's not because she did this." He said. "She was the one that really helped me understand a lot of things when I was goin' through some stuff right after I moved up here." He added as they sat down in the living room.

"And that's what I'm tryin' to figure out, why is it that things always happen to us when we come up here from St. Louis?" She asked him. "It started with Douglas when he left home and moved up here and I just don't get it."

"It's not so much because it's here but it's the people that had an effect on us." Michael told her. "Douglas met Irene up here and that's how he hooked up with her mother and it's kind of a domino thing, you know what I mean?"

"I'm tryin' to get it and this thing with Terry, I'm really a little skeptical Michael." She said, shaking her head a little. "And when David finds out about this, he's really gonna blow up, I'm warnin' you honey."

"What are you skeptical about?"

"I don't really understand all of that that went on with her but Michael she's not gonna all of a sudden switch gears from what

97

she's used to doin.'" She said. "That just doesn't happen, she's gonna probably need some counselling and a lot of other stuff before she's able to beat that because it's an addiction, just like a drug that you have to have."

"I'm sure it is, I'm not doubtin' any of that but when you have the power of God, stuff like that is not gonna beat you." He told her. "Have you ever had the chance to talk to Douglas about how the Lord got him out of his drugs and alcohol?"

"I think I remember him tryin' to tell me about that when he first started goin' to church up here but that was so long ago, I don't really remember much about what he said." She reluctantly admitted.

"The same thing that happened to us was what you saw Sunday with Terry and after what she went through, I don't see her goin' back to that."

"Just mark my words Michael, it's all good right now but give her a month or two, and if she's stayin' up here, it probably wouldn't hurt if you and Douglas look into some places where she can get some help." She concluded. "So what are you gonna do in here, flip it and make it look like they do on t.v.?" She said as she purposely changed the subject.

"We're gonna knock down a couple of walls and put laminate down all over the floors but other than that it'll be pretty much the same."

"So will Janice be movin' in here with you?"

"If and when we say I do but not before." Michael said after a moment, expecting a negative reaction from her.

"It's that way huh?"

"It's that way and I know that's not the way people do things now but I've seen too many messes go down with that shackin' up thing and I'm not goin' there." He said without hesitation or compromise. "No rings, no flings."

"So you're one of those born again virgins I'm assuming?"

"If that's what you wanna call it, that's up to you ma'am." He told her. "And don't get me wrong, I'm still a man and all of that but I'm lettin' my Holy Ghost keep me out of trouble."

"This must be what Terry was talkin' about when she would send me these text messages about you."

"Could've been but it is what it is." "The same thing that happened to her yesterday happened with me a month ago and I can't tell you what a difference that it's made." "I wish I could explain it to you so you would understand but I can't." He admitted.

"I'm glad for you and all of that but like I said, with Terry it's gonna take a lot more than all of this feel good church stuff for her." She said with more skepticism. "Mark my words little brother."

"I don't know if Doris told you or not but she asked me if I wanted to go back to St. Louis with her." Terry remarked that evening on the screened porch with Douglas.

"She ran that by me and I told her it was up to you but I see you're still here." He said as he closed up his laptop.

She nodded a little. "If I went back down there, it would just be too many bad reminders of what I was doin' and I don't need that."

"No, you don't, and whenever thoughts like come to your mind, you have the power now to overcome that stuff."

"It used to be all I would think about but after Saturday night, I don't want anything to do with any of that." "Is that crazy or what?"

"What you went through was enough to turn you off plus you have the spirit of God now that's gonna help you when it tries to come back to you and it will." Douglas told her as he spoke from experience. " It's that way because the Lord is savin' your soul and not your flesh and as long as we're on this earth, there's gonna be a war goin' on between the two but as long as you allow God to help you, there's nothin' that can beat you."

"I think that's what Irene was tellin' me this mornin' 'cause when I woke up, it was like, did I dream all of that?" She said as she wiped tears from her face. "It was like this was too good to be true and then these flashbacks of Saturday night started happenin' and that's when I started thankin' God all over again because they almost took me out Douglas."

"But He said not so and for the rest of your life or until Jesus comes, you'll have that testimony that can help and encourage somebody else so don't ever hesitate to tell about what the Lord did for you." He told her. "And I've seen a lot of people receive the Holy Ghost but there was somethin' different about the way it happened for you that I've never seen before."

"For real?" She asked him.

"When did you start to realize what was goin' on?"

"I was talkin' to Michael one time and he was tellin' me about the day he got it and I remembered him talkin' about how he was talkin' in another language and that's when I knew." She said. "And that's why I had to tell him how much he helped me and he probably didn't even know it 'til yesterday."

"And you did the right thing by lettin' him know that because that encourages you to keep doin' the right thing." Douglas told her.

"I could tell that it was somethin' different in his face the night that you came and got me out of jail." She said as her voice dropped when she thought back to the humiliation of the experience.

"He was just about where you are now and when you go back to work in a couple of days, the people that are used to seein' you look and act a certain way will be able to tell that there's somethin' different about you." "And this is just the beginnin' because if you allow the Lord to change you into what He wants you to be, there's no tellin' how many other people that you can affect just by talkin' about what He delivered you from."

"I can't wait Douglas because this is just too good to not tell somebody else about it." She said as best she could without losing herself in the joy that she was experiencing.

"You'll get your chance honey, just make it up in your mind to be as close to the Lord as you possibly can because that's when He'll use you." He assured her. "Make sure that you get some prayer time in every day and it doesn't matter if you just thank God for allowin' you to see another day in the mornin' when you wake up because none of us is promised the next day when we go to bed at night."

"Tell me about it." She said as she listened intently to him.

"I don't say that to be morbid but you know first hand now what it means to almost check out of here so don't ever take the goodness of God for granted." He said. "And I have two or three extra bibles down there in the office so feel free to go down there and get one of 'em so you can really start to learn what this is all about."

"Michael told me that too so I guess I need to listen to my brothers huh?" She asked him.

"We don't know everything but whenever you feel like you need to talk to somebody, there's plenty of people around here that'll take time with you because nobody makes it through here alone." He admonished her.

"Irene's cousin, is Sheila her name?" She asked him.

"Did you get the chance to talk to her last night?"

"She gave me her phone number and told me that I could call her anytime about anything so that's good to know."

"She's good to talk to because you're pretty much the same age and she's serious about her salvation so get with her as much as you can."

"Do you think that I should apologize to James for that day out here a couple of weeks ago?" She asked him a moment later.

"If you feel like that's what you need to do, he'd be glad to talk to you but I really don't think he's thought a lot about that Terry." Douglas said as he noticed her embarrassment. "That's all in your past but if you think it would free you of somethin' that you feel uncomfortable about, I'll let him know and you can talk to him and Chris together if you want to."

"Have they moved in their new house yet?"

"They moved out there Saturday mornin' so they're still gettin' unpacked and all of that so I would give 'em a couple of days." He said as Janice and Michael came in from outside.

"That was quick, you must not have been that far away." Terry told Michael as she slowly stood up and approached them.

"Doin' okay?" He asked her.

"I think you already know." "I'm still a little sore but I'm gonna make it."

"Yep you are." He told her as he motioned for Douglas to follow him out.

"I wanted to talk to you last night at church but there was a lot goin' on." Janice said as she sat down a moment later after Douglas and Michael went into the house.

"Just too awesome." Terry said, thinking back to the night before. "But I sent Michael a text and asked him to bring you over here but I didn't think he'd get here so quick."

"He was out there workin' in Paul and Jane's house and that's just five hundred steps from us so he just walked over and told me that we were goin' for a ride." Janice said while noticing her discomfort as she sat back down.

"I know, this is my own fault but it's gettin' better." Terry said. "Is it anything we can do or get for you?"

"They just told me to get some rest and Irene's makin' sure that I don't do too much." She began. "But I wanted to talk to you because I've said some things about you just because you're pregnant and your baby isn't Michael's." She managed to say with regret. "It wasn't any of my business and I'm just apologizin.'"

"Are you serious?" Janice asked her, shocked at what she had just said.

She nodded. "And you're not the only one that I have to talk to because I don't think I'll feel right until I do." "Does that make any sense?"

"I knew that you sort of have a problem with it but he never told me anything that you said." Janice said, still trying to comprehend her.

"I'm glad that he didn't but I know myself the things that I said and I wasn't bein' fair about it." She admitted.

"But I don't want you to feel like you owe me an apology because you haven't done anything to me."

"I didn't actually do anything but I said some things and that can be just as bad or worse so I'm just makin' sure that I get this cleared up with you because I don't want anything to get in my way." She said as she found herself already beginning to feel the process of becoming the new creature that the Word of God has spoken of.

"Do you know how much this is helpin' me?" Janice asked her as she began to think about the unfinished business that she had with Kathryn.

"Really?" Terry asked, sincerely puzzled by her reaction.

"You just said somethin' that made me think about how I need to talk to my mother about some stuff that went on and I keep puttin' it off because I don't know how it's gonna go down with her." Janice said. "And I said some things to her right before I got the Holy Ghost a couple of months ago that I said without thinkin' first." She admitted.

"Does she live here?"

"She's in D.C. but some things happened a couple of months ago and we got into it about some stuff." She said, thinking back. "Then when I found out that Irene is my sister instead of my cousin like I thought, that really kind of made it all worse."

"You're sisters?"

"We're half sisters because we have the same father but nobody knew about it 'til he told us right before he died." Janice explained to her. "My mother did of course but she didn't tell me a lot of things that I should've known and when it came out, I was a little messed up because of it."

"I think Irene told me about how you and Douglas have like an understandin' that he's your father figure because of a lot of stuff that happened."

"He is, and James is the brother that I never had so it all worked out because God knows what you need and when you need it." Janice said. "And when I first started comin' to work with him, people would ask me what was up with that and I would just say that's my brother and they would just look at me I was crazy." She said, laughing a little.

"Like how is he gonna be your brother, you're black and he's white huh?" Terry asked her.

"Exactly and they sort of joke about it now but when I started to show, there was this thing goin' around the office that he was the father and it was really crazy for a minute 'til we got 'em straight about it."

"He seems to be really laid back so maybe I shouldn't be afraid to talk to him huh?"

"You shouldn't, he's harmless just like Douglas is and I think that's why they're so tight, their personalities are a lot alike."

"I need to apologize to him too because like I said, I don't want anything from what I did before to get in the way of anything that God wants me to do and I just wanna clear up some stuff." She said with a serious tone in her voice.

"I know what I need to do now, you're already lettin' the Lord use you and it's just been a day." Janice said.

"But I wasn't tryin' to make you feel like that's what you have to do, I'm doin' this because what I was doin' was wrong."

"Don't worry about it because I'm not trippin' about this anymore like I was before; I'm not tryin' to make Michael do anything and he tells me all of the time that if it works out, it's because the Lord did it." She concluded. "And when God does things, it's all good."…

MAY 22, FRIDAY

"I woke up in here Sunday mornin' and it was like I was layin' in a cloud." Frances remarked as she and Michael sat on the deck Friday afternoon after he finished working at Paul and Jane's house. "Couldn't hear a thing and I'm used to hearin' traffic but out here you can almost hear the grass growin'." She added.

"So is that a good or a bad thing?" He asked her, amused at her analogy.

"I think that I'm startin' to like it son and when am I gonna get to meet your sister that was born the other night?" She asked him. "I heard about it but I wanna hear it from her."

"Irene is bringin' her out here later on when Douglas gets home." He said. "She said that she needs to talk to Chris and James and I can't believe some of the things that Janice told me that she said to her the other day."

"She told me that she talked to her and that just goes to show you that it doesn't take the Holy Ghost long to start workin' and from what she said, this girl is gonna be used by the Lord in a big way, you heard it here first." Frances said with confidence. "And Douglas was the same way, he started tellin' people about what happened to him before he had any real knowledge to back up what he was sayin', but when you come close to leavin' here and the Lord steps in just in time and snatches you out of the devil's traps, you can't help but talk about it."

"And if they hadn't gotten to her when they did, she wouldn't have made it."

"But that's how prayer makes all of the difference and I know that you and your brother had to have been doin' some heavy duty prayin' for her." "And the more you do it, the more God will work for you and fight your battles that are too big for you so don't stop now." She told him. "This is just the beginnin' because sometimes when you come out of one thing, here comes somethin' else to try you but the Lord has given you His power so we don't have any excuse when it comes to makin' it through here."

"When you said that about prayer, it made me think about somethin' that I wanted to ask you about."

"I'm listenin' honey, I might not have the answer but I'll give you what God gives me." She said as she opened a small bottle of water.

"Do you ever run out of things to pray about?" He cautiously asked her.

"There might have been a time when that was true but the longer that you walk with the Lord, the longer your prayer time gets." She immediately answered. "And the more people that you meet, the more you'll find yourself interceeding for situations if you love like you're supposed to."

"I was wonderin' about that because I know for a fact that I've heard my brother down there in his office for a good hour goin' at it like it was no tomorrow." He added, laughing and shaking his head.

"Because he's a prayer warrior and that's what it takes to get results." Frances said. "When you have a relationship with the Lord like that, you can believe that person is gonna be used by God but it takes time to get to that place." "You stay with it and you might be the same way in a few years so don't get discouraged and think just because you can only pray for a few minutes that the Lord doesn't hear you." "He'll answer a prayer that takes just a few seconds just like He will those marathon prayers that Douglas does."

"And I'm thinkin', how does he do that for so long?" Michael said. "And I don't mean to be eavesdroppin' or anything like that but there's somethin' about hearin' prayers like that that helps me out and it's not even me doin' the talkin', you know what I mean?"

"Because your spirit is bearin' witness to that same one that he has because it's all one and it can relate if that makes any sense to you."

"It does because I remember when we walked into Terry's hospital room Sunday afternoon and heard her speakin' in tongues and it was unmistakable, we just knew because of the anointing that was in there." "It was awesome and everytime I think about it, I lose it."

"Irene told me about it but like I said, I'm ready to meet her and hear about it from her." She said as Chris came out the sliding door with Jay.

"Feelin' a little better?" Frances asked her as she put him on her lap a moment later.

"I don't feel that bad, I'm just worn out and I just talked to James, he said not to worry about cookin' anything so that's a load off."

"Didn't I tell you not to worry about that, that's what I'm here for honey." Frances told her.

"I know but I don't want you to overdo it either." "When did you sneak over here Michael Johnson?"

"Ten or fifteen minutes ago, I just got done paintin' the last bedroom over there and I came by here to talk to my best friend for a while."

"What time is Terry comin'?"

"Probably around five or six, she's comin' with Irene."

"I really don't want her to feel like she has to come all the way out here for somethin' that's not really necessary, nobody is holdin' anything against her." Chris said. "We know what she did was before so we're not expectin' anything from her."

"But if that's the way the Lord is leadin' her, let her do what she has to do honey." Frances told her. "We might all learn somethin' from her if we take the time to listen to what she has to say."

"She got to Janice, I know that much." Michael said.

"She said that she doesn't really know how to bring all of that stuff up to Kathryn and that's some of the reason why she hasn't called her before now."Chris said.

"Maybe Kathryn needs to call her, you really can't expect Janice to bring that up to her." Frances said, defending her.

"But I think she'll feel better when she gets some stuff out of her system, she's holdin' on to some things that ain't healthy." Michael said after a moment.

"Then you're probably the one that has more influence on her other than Douglas."

"Yeah I was about to say, I'm probably number two on her list right now when it comes to things like that."

"Then maybe they need to have a conversation before she talks to Kathryn because if you keep things in your heart against somebody, your prayers are hindered and nobody needs to go there." Frances said.

"That's pretty deep right there, I didn't know that." Michael said.

"Those are the things that you learn by hangin' around us young man." Frances told him.

"So I see; maybe I need to put a bug in his ear because she's been a little different since she talked to Terry the other day."

"Sort of quiet like?" Chris asked him.

"You noticed that too huh?"

"James did too but he hasn't said anything to her because we're all goin' through right now." Chris said. "This was a big move and all of us are tryin' to get used to it out here and I need to do stuff but I'm just not feelin' it right now." She admitted.

"Anything I can do while I'm just sittin' here?" Michael asked her as he began to text Douglas.

"I have a Honeydo list for James that you can take over if you want to." "Since you offered and all of that good stuff I'm gonna take you up on it."

"Let me have it ma'am, I'm at your service."

"Me and Jane decided to see if we can grow some tomatoes over there by the shed and they have the starter plants on sale at that hardware store up the road." "And crazy 'Nita Scott talked James into buildin' a chicken house so she can sell eggs in a few months."

"Are you serious?" Michael asked, starting to laugh.

"I told her she's been watchin' too many episodes of Lucy because they did the same silly thing but he said he needs about twenty five two by fours to start out with and you can probably get all that at one place."

"So where is she gonna get the chickens from?"

"She found a hatchery on line somewhere and she's plannin' on buyin' some baby chickens so they can grow up and lay eggs." Chris said, laughing with him. "Is that crazy or what?"

"Not for 'Nita Scott, that sounds pretty much like her."

"If she can pull that off, it could lead to other things so give her a chance and see what happens." Frances said. "She could be doin' a lot of stuff that could cause problems so I say let her go for it."

"This is gonna be more fun out here than I thought and that took some imagination even if she did see it on Lucy first." Michael commented. "That might be the start of somethin' big.".

"Irene said for you to eat the rest of these tacos because she made too many of 'em." Douglas said around six-thirty as Michael and Janice sat down at the kitchen table.

"You don't have to tell me twice." Michael said as he took two from the plate. "Chris put me to work out there and I worked up an appetite."

"What did she have you doin'?"

"James' honeydo list."

"Uncle Michael's here!" Ryan said, running upstairs from the basement after hearing him. "Can you come down there and play Uno with us?" "Please?"

"Who else do you see?"

"Can I get a hug?" Janice asked him as he came over to her.

"Are you gonna have a baby?"

She nodded.

"Is it a girl or a boy?"

"It's a girl."

"C'mon dude, let's go play Uno." Michael told him as he and Douglas both noticed her demeanor begin to change which was a signal to him to give them their space.

"You know it's gettin' deep when the kids start to notice things." She remarked after Michael went downstairs.

"But that's not the real issue is it?" Douglas asked her as he sensed her preoccupation with other things.

She shook her head in admittance. "After I talked to Terry the other day, I can't really think about anything else except that I need to call mother and get some stuff straight with her."

"How did that come up?"

"She was apologizin' to me for some stuff that I didn't even know about and I couldn't believe what I was hearin' from her." Janice said.

"Specifics if you can remember." He asked, becoming fascinated. "I'm just tryin' to figure out what's goin' on because we can tell that you're not yourself and if what she said was enough to shake you up like this, it had to be some serious stuff."

"She just said some things that reminded me that I still haven't talked to her about how I got here."

"So that's still botherin' you?"

"I thought that I was mostly over it but it's the way she let me think that he was my father for eighteen years is what I'm havin' a little bit of a problem with." Janice said. "And if that's wrong, I need to know about it so I can get rid of it."

"Are you askin' the Lord to help you with that because sometimes He's the only one that can."

"When we first found out about it I was and then it felt like it wasn't as bad and I sort of kept pushin' it out of my mind." She said after a moment. "Then after Terry said some things, it just all started to come back and it was like I need to take care of this as soon as I can."

"But you don't quite know how to bring it up do you?" He asked as if he were reading her mind.

"I really don't but I know that it's not gonna go away by itself." Janice said. "And I have this feelin' that she's not gonna want to talk about it and I'll be right back where I started out."

"Have you and Marie talked about this?"

"I haven't said anything to her and I'm not even sure if she knows about it."

"There's only one way to find out and you're not gonna feel any better until you let God help you do what you have to do."

She nodded in agreement.

"And you might be surprised at the way she reacts, she may not make a big deal out of it at all but even if she does, you don't have to."He began. "Then if she doesn't feel like she wants to talk about why she didn't tell you, you can't force her into it but you can let her know that you're not holdin' it against her."

"But it has to be the truth and I'm really tryin' to get there because when I think about the difference he made between Marie and me, it hurts Douglas." She said as she let a few unashamed tears fall down her face.

"I know it does honey but even though it hurts, you still have to get to the place where you can forgive her for what she made you go through and move on." He told her with wisdom coupled with compassion for her. "When the Lord gave us the Holy Ghost, that's what He did with all of the stuff and the mess that we got mixed up in so who are we to hold on to things?"

"I can't, you're right." She said after thinking a moment.

"Then when you make up your mind to forget those things that are behind you, you set yourself free and you also get her off the hook as far as the two of you go." He told her. "Does that make sense to you?"

"It does when you put it that way."

"And even more important than that, you don't want the Lord to disregard your prayers because you're holdin' things in your heart against her or anybody else." He commented. "This is serious business and the Lord doesn't want you goin' around feelin' burdened down because of somethin that you didn't have any control over." "He brought you here to start all over again so don't let anything mess that up plus you have to think about your baby." "Right now, she's connected to you and the way you feel can affect her so the best thing you can do is to not let another day go by without doin' what you know is right."

"Have you ever gone through anything like this?" She asked him.

"Not exactly what you're dealin' with but I can remember the first agency job that I got about a year after I got the Holy Ghost and I was workin' with a guy that was supposed to be trainin' me if that's what you wanna call it." He said as he thought back to the experience. "Anyway, to make a long story short, when you're sellin' insurance, you have a quota to make and if you fall short or don't open up enough new policies, they let you go, plain and simple."

"That's pressure."

"It was but this guy knew how to get in the system and for whatever reason, deleted probably about seventy five per cent of the policies that I had sold." "So by the end of the quarter, it looked like I hadn't done enough to keep the job and I got a pink slip with rent and and a car payment to make and no money in the bank."

"Was Irene workin' anywhere?"

"She had a retail job makin' probably six or seven dollars an hour and I was on her crumb list anyway because of church and I have to come home and tell her that I lost my job."

"Wow."

"Put yourself in my place, I'm doin' the best I can tryin' to keep stuff together while the devil is steady tellin' me that I had it better when I was out there sellin' drugs for a livin' and had money to burn." Douglas said.

"That sounds so hard."

"It was, I'm not gonna sit here and tell you that it wasn't but one Sunday night there was a deacon that took me aside because he could tell that I was a little discouraged about the way things were goin.'" He continued. "He sat me down and told me about the scripture that says no weapon formed against you would prosper and how all things work together for good to them that love God, to them that are the called according to His purpose and so and so on." He said. "And it's good when you can quote scriptures but until you actually see for yourself that God can't lie, you can't really help somebody else until you have a testimony for yourself that nobody can take away from you." "But before I went home that night, he handed me an envelope that had a hundred dollar bill in it and back then, that was almost like a thousand because money went a lot further back then than it does now."

"So that's how you got through all of that?"

"This is what happened." He continued. "I got kicked to the curb and got busy and found another job with the help of the Lord but one day out of the blue, I got a phone call from this same guy that was responsible for me losin' the first job that I told you about." "It had been over a year since I had seen him but he still had my phone number and he called me one night at home and told me what he had done because the whole thing had caught up with him." "The district manager found out some kind of way what he had been up to and of course he got fired but he felt so bad about it, he was callin' to ask me to forgive him for what he had done and what choice did I have?"

"None." She answered after thinking a moment.

"You couldn't have said it any better and after all of that, I got a commission check in the mail a couple of weeks later for all of those policies that I had sold and didn't get credit for." Douglas concluded. "You can't go wrong when you do what His word says to do, even if it takes years to see the results of your obedience and you never know how you might affect your mother by doin' what your Holy Ghost is tellin' you to do."

"I don't think I've ever told you how much I appreciate how you've helped me through so much Douglas." Janice said then. "I'm so thankful I don't know what to do."

"And that's how the Lord wants us to be and I can't take credit for anything because if I've been any help to you, it's from God."

"It has to be because every time somethin' comes up, you have all of the answers." She said as she slowly stood up. "Can I go downstairs and use the phone in your office?" She asked him.

"Help yourself ma'am, you know where it is."

"I've been meanin' to call you but things just keep comin' up and I don't remember things like I used to." Kathryn remarked on the phone with Janice ten minutes later.

"Is that because of the accident?"

"It could be but my doctor says that could be temporary and not to worry about it." "But are you doin' okay, have I talked to you since you told me about the baby?"

"I don't think I have." Janice said as she began to feel herself become unnerved at the thought of her reason for calling. "And everything is goin' okay with her, I'm goin' to the doctor once a month."

"Are you callin' to tell me that you're ready to come back home?"

"No ma'am, I can't do that, I've got a lot goin' on here and I don't think I'd be able to make it there anymore."

"So I'm not gonna be able to be close to my grandbaby when she comes?" Kathryn asked with a wounded and disappointed tone to her voice.

"Do you feel good enough to come here?"

"I probably can but I would love for both of you to come back home with me." She insisted. "Since I don't have your father anymore, it gets pretty lonely here without him."

"Did you know that we found out that he wasn't my father?" Janice asked her after a moment as she felt a spirit of boldness come up in her.

"I know that." She said as her voice turned icy cold. "I really didn't want you to ever know that but he went home and opened his mouth."

"But why didn't you want me to know?" Janice patiently asked her. "If you had told me maybe when I was twelve or thirteen years old, then I would've known why he acted different with me than he did with Marie." She managed to say with a degree of nervousness.

"I didn't tell you because it would've caused more trouble than it was worth Janice." Kathryn said then. "He would tell me when he got mad at me about somethin' else altogether that he was gonna tell you just to make me do what he wanted me to do." She said as she began to suddenly feel sorry for herself. "He would hold it over my head so I just never told you and I'm sorry if this has hurt you but you need to try to understand my side of it honey."

"Does Marie know?"

"I never told her either because I was afraid that she might let it slip out and it would've been a big mess."

Then for the first time Janice turned her attention from her own feelings and issues with the situation around to what Kathryn had endured from Roy for eighteen years. She began to feel a degree of selfishness after hearing her version and reasons for keeping the truth from her and immediately felt a release in her spirit as she let go of the unprofitable "hurt feelings" of the past.

"And you know what, now that you just told me what was goin' on, it feels different all of a sudden and I'm just ready to let this go mother." Janice said as she let her emotions and the anointing of her spirit cause her to feel a release that was liberating to them both. "Whatever happened, happened and both of us have to move on from this and I'm not holdin' any of that against you anymore because I have too much to thank God for to be hangin' on to this." She finished through free flowing tears as she felt the approval of the Lord for what she had just done.

"Is Douglas still doin' what he told me he would do for you?" Kathryn asked through her own tears of regret mixed with an unexplicable feeling of relief, like a weight had been lifted from her.

"Yes ma'am, I just got through talkin' to him about this and I'm callin' you from their house."

"Do you think he'll talk to me?"

"He will, can you hang on for a minute?" Janice asked her as she started out of his office with the cordless phone.

"Everything ok hon?" Douglas asked her after she found him out on the screened porch a minute later.

"She wants to talk to you." She said as she handed him the phone and started back out to go sit in Michael's car parked in the driveway.

"Hey Kathryn, how are you?" He asked her after a moment.

"I'm really doin' okay now since I just talked to my baby girl." Kathryn answered after gathering her composure.

"So how did that go if you don't mind me askin.'"

"She kind of took me off guard when she started talkin' about this business with William because I thought all of that was settled and over with." She said.

"From the looks of it, it was but she had some things that she had questions about and she didn't feel like it was really closed out if I can put it that way." Douglas told her. "And that was why she called you because she wanted to find out why she didn't know a long time ago but I think after tonight she feels better about it."

"You know her pretty well don't you?"

"After three months I know pretty much how she thinks and this whole thing has been a blessin' to both of us so it's not a one way street."

"Then that lets me know she's in good hands and since she just told me she doesn't want to come back here, it's good to know that you're lookin' out for her."

"We all are and I make sure that I talk to her once a week at least just to see if everything is okay."

"Then I heard through the grapevine that your brother is a pretty good friend of hers, how true is that?"

"That's pretty accurate and I'm watchin' that too so try not to worry about it, he knows what's up."

"How does he feel about her havin' a baby that's not his?" Kathryn asked him.

"For some reason that's not makin' any difference to him and he seems to be really protective of her so between the both of us, she'll be okay." He assured her.

"I'm gonna hold you to that."

"So how are Marie and Jerry doin', I haven't talked to either one of 'em since she left."

"They're doin' a lot better than they were a few months ago and I think it's because Marie is a lot easier to live with." Kathryn said. "She would always be the one to start things between them and I just don't see that anymore."

"That's a good thing."

"She found a church that she really likes and he hasn't been with her yet, but she said that she keeps rememberin' the stories that she heard about you and Irene and that's one of the things that keeps her goin'."

"Then the next time you talk to her, tell her that I said she'll have her own stories to tell as long as she keeps doin' the right things." Douglas told her. "Sometimes it's hard but it pays off."

"I really do wish I could tell you how bad I feel about that but it was somethin' that I couldn't help." Terry remarked with James and Chris in the family room half an hour later.

"Then why don't we do this." James suggested. "Why don't we just act like it never happened because we don't want you around worryin' about what we think about you and all of that stuff." "How does that sound to you?" He asked.

"It sounds like what I was hopin' you would say." She said, obviously relieved.

"Honey we don't have any choice." Chris told her. "What happened to you last week-end wiped all of that out so why would we keep bringin' it up?" "That would be so wrong because that's not what the Lord does so why would we?"

"And it's not like anything happened, let's keep this real." James said after a moment.

"Do you know when you can go back to work?" Chris asked her, anxious to change the subject.

"I'm goin' back Monday and I got a call from the prosecuter's office and they were askin' me some questions about if I wanted to take all of those guys to court but I just need to forget about the whole thing." She said as Frances and Irene came in. "If I did that, it wouldn't do anything but remind me of all of the stuff I have to get over."

"And the Lord is gonna help you do just that because He has some things that He's gonna do with you." Frances told her as she sat down next to her on the loveseat. "I really can't tell you what it is but I was down prayin' one night earlier this week and I called your name out before the Lord because until you get on your feet and get a really good stronghold in God, you need your strength because things and people are gonna come after you because of what you've been through." She told her as she felt the touch of God confirming what she had just spoken to her.

Terry nodded as she began to be taken in by her words that were perplexing but encouraging at the same time.

"You have a powerful testimony that will help so many other people and whatever you do, don't let anybody else stop you from tellin' about what God has done for you sweetheart." She continued. "And you remind me so much of Douglas right after the Lord gave him the Holy Ghost."

"Really?" Terry asked her as she laughed a little.

"He was unstoppable because he came so close to leavin' here without salvation, and he wanted all of those people that he had been doin' the streets with to know about what happened to him."

"And I had the nerve not to like it and didn't have sense enough to know how much better off he was." Irene commented. "All I could see was that we weren't gonna be doin' all the stuff together that I thought was fun and I didn't appreciate him for it."

"But he didn't let that stop him and that's exactly why the Lord is usin' him right now." "God saw somethin' in him before he saved him which is probably why He didn't allow the devil to take him out and there's a good possibility that it's the same way with you." She told

Terry. "So is there anything that we can do for you since you made the trip all the way out here?"

"I can't think of anything right now but I'm glad that I got the chance to get everything straightened out because I keep feelin' like there's somethin' that God wants me to do but I'm not sure what yet."

"Then what you do is tell the Lord just what you told us and watch and see what happens honey." Frances told her. "This is your new beginning so get yourself ready…

Chapter 7

May 25, Monday

"Did your brother tell you that I was there the night it happened?" Anthony asked Terry Monday afternoon in the store break room before they clocked in for work.

"I think he did tell me that and I haven't gotten the chance to thank-you for everything you did." She said with appreciation as she finished her lunch.

"I tried to call you but I got this message sayin' your number wasn't in service anymore." He persisted.

She nodded. "I learned that from my other brother, he had to do that too."

"Are you sure that you're okay?" "Did somethin' get messed up with you when you were in the hospital?"

"They told me that I got a concussion but I feel okay." "That's why I had to take a week off but I'm better now than I was before all of that happened."

"That's what I'm sayin', are you on some kind of medication or somethin'?"

"I'm not on anything but God gave me the Holy Ghost before I left the hospital and that's why I seem different to you." She told him "Have you ever heard of that?"

"I haven't but maybe my mother has, she goes to church sometimes." He said as he kept staring at her, trying to figure her out.

"Are you doin' anything tonight around seven?" She asked him as she got up to clock in on the computer.

"Not much, what's goin' on?" He asked her with an indifferent shrug.

"I told my brother, the one that you talked to, that I need to talk about what God did for me at his youth meetin' tonight so if you wanna come you can."

"Hold up, you're tellin' me that you're goin' to somebody's church now?" He asked her in total shock.

"I am but this didn't happen when I was at church, I was in the hospital and if you wanna hear about it, you can come around seven." She told him again as they started down the steps to the sales floor. "I'll write the address down for you before I get off and if you come, your pants have to be pulled up.".

"Man when Doris came back here and told me about went down with Terry, I almost drove up there myself with my forty-five for Mister King of the Hill himself." David remarked on the phone with Michael after waking him up."

"What were you gonna do David, end up in jail for shootin' your brother?" Michael asked him after a moment.

"I told Irene when I was up there about a month ago that this would happen to her and nobody wanted to believe it so what does he have to say now?" He asked, ignoring his question.

"There's one way to find that out, he'd probably be glad to talk to you." Michael said calmly, not allowing his words to unnerve him. "And why don't you call Terry, she's the best one to talk to."

"I tried that man and her number is out of service, what's up with that?"

"She got her number changed so she won't have to deal with a lot of people and mess that she did before." Michael began. "And I don't feel right talkin' for her, she went back to work today and she's a lot better off now than she was before, believe me."

"Accordin' to what Doris told me, she was on some kind of religious trip and when she comes back down to earth, she'll be in the same mess again and next time she won't be as lucky." He said.

"If she's gonna stay up there, you and Douglas need to get her into some kind of counselling where she can get some help." "She's sick."

"Do you want her new number?" Michael asked him refusing to argue with him, while giving him the opportunity to talk to Terry himself.

"And what're you gonna do if she ends up pregnant by one of the animals that did this to her?" David spewed out with satanic venom.

"She got treated at the hospital for that but if it happens anyway, we'll deal with it." Michael said, remaining unmoved by his spirit that was determined to throw him off. "And that doesn't mean abortion either." He added.

"Man c'mon what're you talkin' about?" David asked him in frustration. "You would talk her into keepin' a kid that wouldn't know who the heck his father is because his mama is a slut?" "What kind of a trip are you on?" "It's bad enough that you're hookin' up with a girl that's knocked up with somebody else's baby but you're tellin' me that you would let Terry go through that just because of some church crap that she got brainwashed with?"

"I'll talk to you later David, Doris has Terry's new number if you want it." Michael told him. "You woke me up, I need to go back to sleep."..

"When I told my brother that I wanted to do this, it was because I feel like this is what God wants me to say." Terry began that night in front of nearly twenty five youths under the age of twenty that came out to hear the "words of her testimony." "I'm here right now because people were prayin' for me when I was out doin' what I wanted to do and I didn't know how close I was gonna come to dyin' until I was in a situation that I couldn't do anything about." She added as she got a couple of nearby tissues when she felt herself beginning to lose her composure.

"I thought that I was big and old enough to take care of myself and I ended up bein' arrested because I was walkin' the streets and lettin' myself be used up just to make a little money." She continued. "I didn't know it but God was protectin' me when I was doin' all the wrong things and I could've been killed out there." She said with emphasis. "I wouldn't listen to what anybody told me because I was stubborn and I was doin' what I thought was a good time." She said pausing and allowing her spirit to speak to her. "My brothers would talk to me about how dangerous it was for me to be livin' like I was but I wasn't listenin' because I thought I knew everything." "They were tryin' to warn me because they loved me and didn't want anything to happen to me because I wasn't ready to die." She added as she noticed the impact that her words were beginning to have on some of those that were intently listening to her.

"Then nine days ago, I went to a party with one of the guys that I work with." "I didn't know anybody else that was there but I thought that it was the thing to do to get to know people." She said pausing again. "I sat down next to somebody that I had never seen before in my life and told him that I was available if he wanted to go have a little bit of fun." She said, shaking her head in shame and regret. "I was sick and before I knew it, he got four other people together and locked me up in this room and they almost killed me." "They were beatin' and rapin' me at the same time and laughin' about it and all of a sudden it wasn't fun anymore." She said as she purposely raised her voice for emphasis. "I felt myself about to pass out because one of 'em slammed my head up against the wall and all I could do was start yellin' and cryin' for them to stop what they were doin' because it wasn't fun anymore." She purposely repeated. "I woke up in the hospital with a concussion and I heard one of the nurses that were takin' care of me say that if I hadn't gotten there when I did, I wouldn't have made it." "I would've died because I didn't listen to people that cared about me." She said as Sheila stood up and went over to a fourteen year old girl who had suddenly become overcome at what she had heard from Terry.

At that, she looked at Douglas who was sitting on the back row as he encouraged her to keep talking despite the somewhat intense content of her testimony.

"They gave me a shot to calm me down and while I was in intensive care, I went to sleep and I started to see things that God was showin' me." She continued. "I felt myself fallin' into some kind of hole and I was yellin' and screamin' at all of these horrible things that I was seein." She said as she recalled the vision of eternal damnation that the Lord had allowed her to see. "I used to think that when you die, then that was it, you just die and that was the end of it." She said with unbridled boldness. "God let me see where I would've ended up because I didn't listen to the truth from people because I was stubborn and I didn't think it mattered what I did because I was old enough to do what I thought was makin' me happy." "Nobody could tell me anything and I almost left here but God gave me one more chance to get it right." "I started beggin' Him to help me because I was layin' there in so much pain, my whole body was hurting, and I started to remember some of the things that my brothers had told me about God's power to do anything." She persisted as she allowed her spirit to have its freedom to speak.

"I didn't deserve God's help but I started tellin' Him about how sorry I was for all of the horrible and disgusting things that I had let myself do with anybody that would pay me a little bit of money." She said with sincere revulsion. "I told Him how sorry I was for gettin' rid of two babies that I got pregnant with that I didn't know who the fathers were and do you know what?" She asked her audience. "He heard every word that I got the strength up to say because as soon as I let Him know that I was done with all of that, I started to hear myself begin to say words that I didn't understand, I was talkin' in some other language that I had never heard before and I couldn't make it stop." "He gave me the Holy Ghost right there in that hospital bed and nobody can ever tell me that there's nothing to this because I know for myself what He did for me." She said as she suddenly let go and let God speak through her once again, blessing her once more with His powerful presence.

As Douglas came up then after seeing that she was basically done speaking for the moment, he put his arm around her and began to take over where she left off while he waited for her "standing ovation" to subside.

"That was a little more than I expected but when God gets in your testimony, anything can happen." He told the young audience as he wiped his eyes with a handkerchief. "My Lord and my God." He added as she held on to him for support. "And I think that this is just the beginning." He said as he picked up the small microphone. "I don't want anybody in here to be hell scared into salvation but if you don't have the Holy Ghost yet, now is the time to ask the Lord to give it to you because nobody in here is promised tomorrow." "You don't have to be old to leave this life and her story is just an example of the mercy and grace of God young people." "She told you about how the Lord spared her life and if it helps just one of you, it'll be worth it and if anybody has any questions or would like to talk to her one on one, I'm sure she'll take the time with you." He said as she quickly nodded in agreement as she took the microphone back from him.

"Before I finish, I just need to say one more thing." She said as she gathered her thoughts. "Before I moved up here from St. Louis a little over a month ago, I don't think that I had ever been to church in my life and Douglas and Michael can tell you, it was the same way with them." "Our parents never took us or really told us anything about God or any of that so this is all new to me so if we can help each other, it'll be a good thing." She finished as tears flowed freely down her face. "And thank-you for listenin' to me."…

May 29, Friday

"You probably wasn't expectin' to see me here were you sweetheart?" David asked Terry after he walked up to the store office where she was working Friday afternoon.

"You're right, I wasn't." She said, sincerely surprised to see him. "When did you get here?"

"Just got off the road, what time do you get off?" "I need to talk to you." He said, coming right to his point.

"I get off in half an hour." She said after glancing at her watch. "How long are you gonna be here?"

"Just over the week-end, I called Michael last night to let him know that I was comin' so here I am baby girl." "Let me take you to dinner if you don't have any other plans."

"I'm not doin' anything, are you stayin' with Michael?"

"That's the plan because I need to see him too." "I'm stayin' away from Douglas right now because I don't wanna hurt him." "I'll be outside waitin' on you." He added as he walked away from the window.

"So what did Doris tell you when she got back home?' Terry asked an hour later after she and David had been seated at the restaurant.

"What if you tell me happened and then I'll let you know the answer to that." He said as he stared intently at her, unable to figure out the difference that he noticed in her demeanor.

"I went to a party with one of my coworkers that night after work and got messed up." She said without hesitation. "I said somethin' stupid to a guy that I had never seen before and he had some friends that he got together and I got locked up in a room with 'em and they almost killed me, I'm not kiddin.'" She said as the waitress walked up to their table.

"Can I get you something to drink?" She asked as she put the menus down in front of them.

"I'll take sweet tea." Terry said after a moment.

"Hey that reminds me, you just turned twenty one didn't you?" David asked her. "You wannna go over there to the bar and celebrate hon?" He asked her. "You're legal now." He reminded her.

She shook her head as she started looking at the menu.

"Didn't you tell me a couple of months ago that you couldn't wait 'til you turned twenty-one so you could drink any time you wanted to?"

"I probably did say that but that was then and this is now David, things are different." She told him as she made eye contact with him.

"So that tells me that you've really let Douglas rub off on you haven't you?"

"He's helped me through some stuff but it's a lot deeper than that and I really can't make you understand what I'm talkin' about." She told him. "And I remember sayin' stuff to Michael when I first moved up here just like you're doin' with me and it's the same thing."

"So he didn't have anything to do with what you say happened to you?" "This church thing that Doris told me about." He said as he persisted in trying to turn her against him.

"I don't know what she said but I know what happened to me and it's a whole lot more than that." She came back. "When I was layin' there in that hospital bed I talked to God for the first time in my life David." She added as she began to repeat her testimony once more, not to be stopped by his arrogance and unbelief.

"What did you tell Him?" He asked her with a sarcastic air that she quickly sensed and responded by boldly answering him with the truth that could not be denied.

"I laid there in all of this pain because nothin' they gave me was workin' and I told God how sorry I was for all of the stuff that I had done and it was like as soon as I said that I was done with all of that, that's when He gave me my help." She said without hesitation. "Have you ever heard of the Holy Ghost David?" She asked him then.

He didn't say anything but shook his head slightly as he continued to try to "read "her.

"I hadn't either but when they showed up in St. Louis and got me out of jail because I was doin' my stupid thing down there, I could tell right away that there was somethin' different about Michael." She told him. "He was a hot mess just like me when he left back in April and he tried to explain to me what had happened to him and he couldn't because 'til it happens to you, you just can't."

"I don't understand what you're talkin' about but you're tellin' me that all of this what you're talkin' about is gonna stop you in your tracks cold turkey, just like that." He asked her as the waitress sat their drinks down in front of them.

"It doesn't really matter what I'm tellin' you because anybody can talk David." She came right back as she remembered Douglas' counsel to her to never try to prove to anyone what she now had possession of.

"So you're tellin' me that the next time you get the chance to do what you're used to doin', you're gonna turn it down now?" He persisted. "Keep it real for me."

"Of course and you know what?" She asked him as she continued to look through her menu.

"Tell me about it."

"I was at work last night and one of the first guys that I met after I moved here showed up about an hour before I got off." She began. "And he had tried to call me but I got my number changed right after I got out of the hospital."

He didn't say anything but continued to listen and watch her.

"And I knew what he wanted because he tried to give me a fifty dollar bill and told me that he'd be back in an hour to pick me up after I got off." She continued as she shook her head a little at the thought. "So after I told him that I wasn't available anymore, he looked at me like he couldn't believe it."

"How old was this guy?"

"He's probably in his thirties somewhere but when I first met him, he told me that he was married but he was separated and he was just in it for the convenience." "And I didn't have a problem with that, I didn't care if he was married or not, I needed the money."

"So just like that you turned him down without a problem." David said with more skepticism.

"I couldn't hardly believe it myself but I know now what I have and one night last week before I went back to work, Douglas sat me down and showed me in the bible just what happened to me and I understand it a whole lot better than I did before." Terry said as she began to tear up. "It's just awesome David and I wish you would believe me."

"So you and Douglas have gotten pretty close since you've been here huh?" He asked her, attempting to change the subject.

"Yeah we have and all of the stuff that you told me about him just isn't true David." She told him. "You had me scared of him but he's nothin' like you said he was."

"You were too young to remember him before he left St. Louis and if you ask him, he'll tell you why they used to call him Junkyard Dog." He said as the waitress came back to take their orders.

"Irene told me some stuff about him and that was some of the reason that I was startin' to believe some of the things that Michael was tellin' me."

"I'll have the babyback ribs dinner." He said quickly, anxious to get back to their conversation.

"I'll take the chicken tenders platter with a side salad." Terry said as she closed the menu.

"And will this be one check or two?"

"Put it all on one, I've got this." David told her.

"You really don't have to do that but thanks anyway." Terry said then.

"It's all good, don't worry about it." He said after a moment. "And what you were sayin' sounds good and all of that but I just need for you to tell me how you got in that situation in the first place darlin'." "I thought Douglas was supposed to lookin' out for you and if he can't do any better than that, he's not the man I thought he was."

"He doesn't have anything to do with what I let happen." "That was my stupidity and he's done more than what I expected so you can't put that on him."

"Mr. can't do no wrong Douglas huh?" He persisted.

"Nobody is sayin' that, but I can't blame anybody but myself for what happened and if he and Michael and Irene hadn't been prayin' for me, I'd probably be dead and I'm so serious when I say that." Terry said, unmoved by his sarcasm. "And I know that you've never heard me talk like that before but if you stick around, you're gonna hear and see me do a lot of things that you're not used to."

"Too bad that I have to be back in St. Louis by Monday mornin' huh?" He asked, obviously making a mockery of her last statement.

"I can't blame you for not believin' anything that I'm sayin' but it just doesn't matter David." She told him as she stirred in the glass of tea with her straw. "I can't get upset with you because I was the exact same way that you are about this but that was before I went to hell and nobody can tell me that I didn't." She added without flinching.

"Are you sure that you just weren't dreamin' Terry?"

"I couldn't sleep so how could I be dreamin?" "I was in too much pain to even think about goin' to sleep, even after they gave me a shot to knock me out for a few hours." She recalled. "I laid there and felt myself fallin' down a dark hot hole and I was wide awake so I know that I wasn't dreamin'." She repeated.

David didn't speak then as he attempted to cover his discomfort with her choice of words but reluctantly allowed her to keep talking.

"And I was layin' there cryin' like a baby and I can't remember the last time that I actually cried about anything." She continued. "I thought that I had it all together and there was nothin' that I wouldn't do because I was so stuck on myself and didn't care who got hurt because of what I did." She said as she shook her head at the thought of what she had been delivered from."

"And that's just the way your favorite brother was and that's why I would say the things that I did about him." David said, referring to Douglas.

"But that doesn't have anything to do with now and like you said, I was too young to remember all of that." She answered. "And if he hadn't laid out the truth to me, I might've still been out there on the street doin' my thing but like Michael told me one time, everybody has a breakin' point."

"So when I talk to him, is he gonna have a story too?" He asked her, purposely redirecting her conversation.

"That'll be up to him and if you ask him, he's not playin' around either."

"What do you mean by that?"

"I mean he's serious as a heart attack about livin' exactly the opposite of the way he used to."

"Does that mean that he has to hook up with somebody that's pregnant with a kid that's not his?" He asked her.

"That's up to him too and if that's what he wants to do, I don't think anybody is gonna make him change his mind about it." Terry told him.

"When I see him later on, I'm really gonna have to get in his head because I know what that's all about." David said. "When I married Sharon, I had no idea how much hell she was gonna put me through just because she needed somebody to help take care of her kids." He said with disgust. "It's hard enough when it's your own but when you think that you're gonna feel the same way about somebody else's, you're makin' a huge mistake." "And by the time I get done with him,

I guarantee you he's gonna have some second thoughts about goin' down that road." "And you heard it here first."…

May 30, Saturday

"The inspection is Monday mornin' at ten and it usually takes two or three days for everything to be finalized so anytime after that, there's nothin' to stop you from movin' in." James remarked as he and Jane walked through their house Saturday morning.

"And this doesn't even seem real James, they're not gonna know how to act with all of this space." She said as they slowly walked from room to room.

"Are you gonna be able to keep up with all of 'em in here, they might be able to find places to hide once they get used to the floorplan."

"We were talkin' about that a couple of days ago so we're gonna sit 'em down and get some stuff organized before we even move in here." Jane said as they stopped in the kitchen and sat down at one of the islands. "So what's your first couple of weeks been like since you moved out here?"

"I think once we get used to how quiet it is and how dark it is at night we'll be okay." "And it's really good to have mother there all of the time and she told Chris that she'll be over here too when she runs out of stuff to do."

"The kids are gonna love that and Paul is already talkin' about maybe gettin' her a car so she can escape if she wants to." Jane said, laughing a little. "So what's goin' on with you, I can tell somethin' is so you might as well get it out of your system." She added.

"I just happened to think about the last time I was in here with your mother; did she say anything to you about that?"

"Yeah she did, she wanted to know why I didn't tell her that you were married to Paul's sister and she should've known better than to ask me that."

"And you know it but how did it come up?" James asked her.

"She called me later on that day and I could tell that somethin' was wrong right away." Jane began. "And I love her and we would do anything for her but this problem that she has is where we part company." "But anyway, she came at me like I was ten years old and told me that she found out somethin' that made her really disappointed in me for not bein' up front with her."

"Are you serious?"

"It didn't click at first and I'm thinkin', what is she talkin' about?" She continued. "So I just let her keep talkin', then she cuts to the chase and says you just let me give James twenty-five thousand dollars that he's gonna waste on his colored wife and kids." She said, quoting her. "James she was hot and I almost hung up on her but my Holy Ghost stopped me at the last second." She said, shaking her head and laughing at the moment.

"So she told you that she was gonna do that?" James asked her.

"Yeah she did and she asked me not to tell you because she wanted to surprise you with it and I didn't think anymore about it." She said, thinking back. "So what was I supposed to say, oh by the way, did you know that James is Paul's brother-in-law?"

"This is crazy." James said as he continued to listen to her.

"Tell me about it so instead of hangin' up on her like I started to, I told her to calm down because number one, that doesn't have anything to do with it and number two, it's not gonna be wasted." She continued. "Then she said somethin' about how my father would turn over in his grave if he knew that she had just blown twenty-five thousand dollars of his money on those people that don't know to manage their finances." "And she went on and on 'til I finally just told her that I was through talkin' about it because she wasn't listenin' to anything I said anyway so I was done." "I changed the subject and started talkin'about somethin' else altogether because she was wastin' her time and energy on me."

"I was just walkin' her through our house over there and she gets this envelope out of her pocket and when she handed it to me, I thought maybe it would be a couple of hundred dollars."

"Believe me, she won't miss it and she'll just write it off on her taxes." Jane told him. "But keep talkin, I wanna know what you did because I can tell you're startin' to feel guilty about somethin.'"

"You know me too well."

"I haven't known you since you were ten years old for nothin' James, come on out with it love." She said as they laughed at the same time.

"She asked me if I had a housekeeper hired to come in and help with the house because that's why they're here, for us as she put it." He began. "And right after she said that, my first thought was to let her have it in her mouth but like you said, my Holy Ghost stopped me in my tracks because nothin' irritates me more than stuff like that." "But right after she started talkin' like that, I had to tell her that I was married to Paul's sister and I'm not kiddin' you, she turned another color Jane." "And there was somethin' about that, that felt like revenge and I know that can't be right." He confessed.

"But it was the truth and she needed to know that this is the twenty first century, those days are gone forever." "But it bothers Chris when you have reactions like that so you have to think about that too."

"Has she said anything about that to you recently?"

"It's been a couple of years maybe but she doesn't want your kids to start noticin' stuff and believe me they pick up on stuff when they're four and five years old."

"Tell me about it, Chris took Patti and Stephen to the school where they're goin' to this fall to get 'em registered and the secretary looked at her and told her that a parent would have to come and get her's done."

"Patti's you mean?"

He nodded. "Stephen looks just like Chris so it wasn't a problem with him but just because she doesn't look anything like her, somebody just assumed that she wasn't her mother and it's things like that that make somethin' come up in me that's not pretty." He admitted.

"But here's what you have to remember James." Jane said. "There are always gonna be people like that as long as we're here in this world and nothin' changes that in us but the Lord." "I was sort of trippin' over somethin' like one time and I happened to be talkin' to Douglas about it and this was probably six or seven years ago."

"Here comes somethin' deep, let me have it."

"It's not really even that deep but it's the truth." She said. "He told me because God is colorblind, we'd better be if we expect to make it out of here without spot or wrinkle." "And that stayed with me until I got to the place where I started lookin' beyond what people look like and try to see 'em as the Lord does." "We have to see the souls of people, not the skin color."

"Shut my mouth." James said then.

"And when you think about it, is it worth it to let stuff like that take your peace?" "You'll make yourself miserable worryin' about what they're sayin' and doin' because of the race thing when the most important thing is how you're handlin' yourself." She told him. "And you know somethin' else that I found out?"

"I'm listenin.'"

"Until you get to the place where this isn't affectin' you, things are gonna keep comin' up to try you 'til you get it right so you might as well get it together and let God help you." She told him with a spirit of love behind her words.

"Yes ma'am, I hear you. He said as they stood up to walk out of the house. "Just don't forget to pray for me."

"Absolutely, can't make it without it."

"Do you have a few more minutes before you have to get back home?" James asked her a minute later as he locked the door behind them.

"Yeah I do, what's up?"

"Chris and mother wanted you to stop in before you go back home."

"Has she been to the doctor yet?"

"She has an appointment next week, I think her and Janice have the same doctor." He said as they started to walk the five hundred steps.

"How does it feel to be livin' with two pregnant people?"

"It's all good, I'd rather have it too full than empty, it's all good."

"So are you ready for this, it's another world out here." Chris commented five minutes later after they walked into the house.

"Like yesterday, I was just tellin' James that it doesn't even feel real but by this time next week, we'll be out here if everything goes like it's supposed to." She said as she followed her into the family room where Janice, Nita and Frances were organizing nearly fifty boxes of new household items that they had purchased for she and Paul for the new house.

"Okay ma'am, come and get it, this is all yours." 'Nita told her as she suddenly stopped in shock at what she had just said. "I got the list of everything right here so you'll know just what you have." She said as she waved a piece of notebook paper that listed the contents of the boxes.

"We talked to Paul first before we got anything so we would know what you needed so have at it honey, you deserve it." Frances told her as they embraced after she quietly let her tears come.

"I just couldn't take all of the money that your mother gave us so we decided to split it right down the middle, that's just fair." Chris told her after 'Nita handed her the list that included fifty bath towels, one hundred washcloths, twenty five twin sheet sets, five hundred rolls of toilet tissue, twenty five rolls of paper towels, twenty five bottles of laundry detergent, twenty five bottles of body wash, one bread making machine, ten cookie sheets, two cookware sets and twenty twin quilt sets.

"We didn't spend the whole twelve thousand so this is what's left." James said as he handed her a check for the balance.

"I really don't know what to say because thank-you just doesn't seem like enough." She managed to say as she hugged them both. "And I almost said that I'm not gonna have enough room for all of this so I forgot that quick where we're gonna be in a few days."

"And you know that this is how the Lord works so you shouldn't really be surprised should you?" Frances asked her. "So just keep bein' thankful and He'll do the rest.

"So am I gonna get to meet your lady friend before I leave tomorrow?" David asked as he and Michael sat at the breakfast nook around eleven thirty.

"I'd have to check with her first, she may have some stuff goin' on and I don't want her to be put in a place where she has to defend herself." Michael told him as he poured juice in a glass.

"And that tells me that you don't care enough about her to keep her out of a situation that both of you might be sorry about later on." David told him. "I was probably about your age when I got involved with practically the same stuff and I found out the hard way that she was in it just to have somebody take care of her kid after the baby's daddy cut out on her." "What makes you think she's not doin' the same thing man?" "Think about it and keep it real."

"Okay, we're gonna back up a minute David." Michael patiently began. "I'm not takin' anything for granted when it comes to Janice and I'm pretty sure that she's not either so before you go there, don't jump to any kind of conclusions."

"But this is how it starts, believe me." "You start out as friends then you take it to the next level and before you know it, you're hooked and trapped before you know what's happenin' to you."

"And that's where you're wrong, no such thing as takin' it to the next level with her and I'm surprised Doris didn't let you know that about me while she was at it."

"You got to be kiddin' me man." He said, staring at him in disbelief.

"Like I told her, I don't have any apologies to make for that and I don't expect either one of you to understand why Terry and me have left that behind until we're married people."

"And I'll believe that when I see it too, I had dinner with her last night and the way she was talkin' just let me know what a job both of you have let Douglas do on you."

"Can you tell me why everything has to come back on him David?" Michael asked him.

"Because I don't think it's any accident that both of you all of a sudden feel like you have to be on this church trip after you move up here and start hangin' around him." "That's not a coincidence, I don't care what anybody says about it."

"And that's up to you but just for the record, he didn't do anything except tell the truth and that was because I was the one that went there with him." "From the first day that I got here, he never brought it up but all I had to do was watch what he would do or not do, and it was Irene's mother that had more to do with what happened to me."

"She's the one that sold you this place for a dollar huh?"

"She's the one and I was sittin' just about where you are now havin' a king sized pity party about my situation and she was the one that took time with me and just about introduced me to the Lord, I'm not kiddin' you."

"Is that when you got your religion or somethin'?" David asked him.

"I didn't get religion, God gave me the Holy Ghost when I finally got to the place when I realized how nothin' I really was." "There's a big difference."

"How did you hook up with her, it's not like you to hang around anybody over thirty."

"The day after I got here, Douglas took a day off from work and we were just goin' around lookin' at who was hirin.'" "And we stopped by here and this is the lady that grabbed me and gave one of the best hugs that I had had in my life, and you just don't forget things like that." "It was real and she had never seen me before that day and we've had this connection ever since that I really can't explain."

"Where is she now, maybe I need to see this person that straightened you out." He said, laughing a little.

"She moved out to the country with Irene's sister and her husband and kids so I don't get to see her as much as I did before."

"How far out are you talkin' about, ten or twenty miles from here?"

"It's about half an hour from here but if I call them and tell 'em that we're comin', don't start anything with Janice because she lives out there too." Michael warned him.

"Just one big happy family huh?"

"I'm serious man because I don't want anything happenin' that might get back to Douglas and believe me, you don't wanna go there."

"What is that supposed to mean?"

"Things happened when she moved here from D.C. a few months ago and as far as she's concerned, Douglas is her father and when I say that, he doesn't take that lightly." "At all." He emphasized.

"And how old is she?"

"She's eighteen and I know you're about to do some math so let me save you the trouble." Michael told him. "He's old enough to be her father and there's nothin' off goin' on."

"That's really interesting, how does her biological father feel about that?"

"They buried him a few weeks ago so that's not an issue and if you're tryin' to find somethin' wrong with that, it's a little too late."

"That just seems a little off character for him but maybe I don't know him like I thought I did."

"Probably not but I'm just tryin' to stop trouble before it starts David." He said as he started to call James. "Give me a minute."

"I can't tell you how excited I was when James told me that you were comin' out here." Frances remarked an hour later as she and David sat down at the patio table on the deck.

"Yeah I was a little surprised when he came to the door, Michael didn't tell me everything."

"Don't let that throw you off, it's all good." Frances said. "So did you just come up here from St. Louis for the week-end?" She asked him as he opened a can of pop.

"Yes ma'am, I heard about what happened to Terry and I had to come and see about her."

"But you know what, she's in good hands now and you have no more reason to worry about her." "I met her for the first time about a week ago and she's gonna be exactly like Douglas, she has a wonderful testimony and she won't be stopped from tellin' people about what God did for her and I can't wait to see her blossom."

"Yeah I took her out to dinner last night and she tried to tell me about some stuff that happened to her that I didn't understand but she seems to have it together for right now."

"It sounds like you don't believe in what the power of God will do son." Frances told him.

To that he had no answer as he was taken aback by her referral to him as her son.

"You know how Douglas became a new creature don't you?" She asked him without hesitation. "God didn't make a mistake when he saved him and it's the same with her so don't ever doubt what He's done."

"Do you remember him when he was actin' a complete fool out there on the streets?"

"He kept me on my knees from the first time he came to pick Irene up on that motorcycle that almost killed him." Frances began. "He came to the door and blew cigarette smoke in my face before he said a word and I almost panicked." She said laughing in retrospect. "This is who was about to take my baby out to Lord knows where and I heard Him tell me in my spirit not to be afraid and I started to get a sense of peace about it but that didn't stop me from prayin' day and night about him."

"So you think that's what turned him around huh?"

"We all know what made him come to himself but there's no such thing as too much prayer." And through that whole thing with him, the Lord taught me how to look beyond all of the corruption and know that there was a soul underneath all of that devilment that needed salvation." She said as she began to tear up at the thought. "And that goes for every last one of us, you're no better than he was just because you've never lived the lifestyle that he did but we're all born in sin and all of need His spirit to make it out of here when He comes back."

"You don't bite your tongue do you?" David asked her after a moment.

"Baby I can't because it's too late in the day to be holdin' back the truth just because somebody might get offended about what I say." "And I don't say anything unless the Lord gives it to me and it's all about lovin' you, even though I never laid eyes on you before ten minutes ago."

"Michael told me about you, I should've listened to him." David said, shaking his head a little.

"Bless his heart, I love him to death and he's comin' along too, so whatever you do, never look at your two brothers and your sister like they're crazy because they get it." Frances told him. "They're runnin' for their lives because it's all about where you spend eternity." She added as Chris came out with Byron.

"He's in there walkin' around lookin' for you." She said as she handed him over to her. "Hey, you're David, right?" She asked him then.

"The one and only." "Are you sure that you and Irene aren't twins?"

"We get that sometimes, like Michael and Douglas." She said as she sat down at the table.

"Where is he anyway, did he cut out on me?"

"Him and Janice went out to lunch somewhere, he hasn't been here in a couple of days so it was time."

"This is quite the layout and Michael told me you've only been out here for a couple of weeks."

"Two weeks ago today so we're still gettin' used to things." "How long are you gonna be here?"

"I'll be headin' back tomorrow sometime, I just had to come up here to see how Terry was, I had to see for myself that she was doin' okay."

"She is, they're makin' sure that she's movin' on and I've never seen anybody else that's been any more vocal than she has so quick."

"About what exactly?"

"She's already got a call from another church to come and talk to the high school kids about what happened to her and she is on top of it, big time."

"Do you remember what I said the first time she came out here to talk to you and James?" Frances asked her. "It was easy to see and from here on out, watch what God does"…

CHAPTER 8

JUNE 2, TUESDAY

"If I had known how much of a difference just that few minutes of talkin' to her was goin' to make, I would've done it a long time ago and saved myself a lot of stress." Janice remarked Tuesday evening in the livingroom with Chris and Donna as she sat holding Sara.

"So you just decided to call her because you hadn't talked to her about it since you found out about the whole thing?" Donna asked her.

She nodded. "I kept puttin' it off and a couple of days after Terry got out of the hospital, she called Michael and told him that she needed to talk to me and I had no idea what was goin' on with that."

"That's different."

"It was, but he took me over there and I sat down with her out on the porch and she started apologizin' to me for some stuff that I didn't even know about."

"Are you serious?"

"I am so serious and I started to feel bad because here she was with the Holy Ghost for two days talkin' like that and I should've done the same thing a long time ago with mother."

"So is that when you called her?"

She shook her head. "I was too busy tryin' to think of what to say to her and how I was gonna bring it up and I just kept sittin' on it." She admitted. "But it wasn't lettin' me alone and Michael could tell that I wasn't myself and that's when he called Douglas and told him that he needed to talk to me."

"That did it huh?" Chris asked as she stood ironing window treatments for Donna.

"And you know it." "He told me some stuff that made me so uncomfortable that I went down in his office and called her before I went back home to get it off of me."

"What kind of stuff if you don't mind tellin' me what he said." Donna asked her, fascinated.

"He said some things that I already sort of knew about but when he started talkin' about the Lord not hearin' your prayers when you're holdin' somethin' against somebody in your heart, that's when it really got deep." She said with regret.

"Yeah that's the first reason you can't do that."

"I know that now and I hope I never forget it but then when he said somethin' about lettin' all of that stuff go, and that it would free both of us up, somethin' clicked, you know what I mean?"

"It does, I remember when all of that mess was happenin' with James' mother." Chris began. "And it wasn't 'til Jane sat me down one night and talked to me like Douglas talked to you, that I forced myself to let it go; I wasn't gonna be bound and messed up because of that ignorance."

"James told me about that and I couldn't believe how different I felt after I told her that it just didn't matter anymore."

"But how did you bring it up, I don't think I would've had the nerve Janice." Donna told her.

"It came up when she asked me if I was callin' to tell her that I was ready to come back home and I just had to tell her that I have too much goin' on here to do that.

"That probably didn't go over too well did it?"

"It didn't, then she told me how lonely it was without my father and that was my chance." Janice said, quoting Kathryn as she remembered the conversation.

"Then she didn't know that we had told you?"

"She didn't, I think she thought that Aunt Frances wasn't gonna tell me what was goin' on." "It doesn't matter anymore but I think she was surprised that I knew."

"Did you ask her why she didn't tell you a long time ago?"

"I did and she explained to me that it might've caused some more problems because he was always throwin' it up to her so she just decided to keep quiet about it." "Marie doesn't even know it so it is what it is but the best part about it, the Lord gave me what I need and it's all good." She said as she handed Sara back to her. "Is she gettin' hungry?"

"It's been a couple of hours, probably so."

"Question Janice and you don't have to answer this if you don't want to." Chris told her then.

"Uh oh, what did I do?"

"You didn't do anything but we were wonderin' if she might be willin' to move here and stay in an assisted livin' place so she could be close to you and the baby and she wouldn't be by herself like she is in D.C." Chris said as she finished with a panel.

"I didn't even think about that."

"That was mother's idea and it might work if she knows that that's the only way she'll be able to keep her hands on Kristen."

"You've already named her?" Donna asked.

Janice nodded. "She's Kristen Marie and I'm about half way through this so it's gettin' a little scary."

"It's nothin' to be scared of but you're gonna be in some pain 'til they help you out."

"I know, Irene got me a book to read so I sort of know what's gonna be happenin'."

"Who do you want in there with you?" Chris asked her.

"I'm not sure yet but if I can talk her into comin' here, she might be okay with it."

"There's one way to find out and it might be a good idea to start now to give her time to think about it." "Four months is not that far off."..

"They want me to go downtown and pick those five guys out of a lineup but I don't remember what they looked like and I don't wanna get anybody in trouble that wasn't there." Terry remarked with Ruth and Sheila at a restaurant after leaving church.

"Is there any way to get out of it and not have to go at all?" Ruth asked her.

"I need to find out because I just don't wanna go there, that's all behind me and I don't want any reminders." She said. "I have too many other things that need to be done to be worried about that stuff.

"So do you know when you're goin' over to talk to the kids at the church that called you?" Sheila asked her as they looked at the menus.

"Sunday at seven and I'll probably have a car by then." "Michael's takin' me to a couple of dealers tomorrow that he knows about so I won't have to bother anybody for a ride over there."

"How did they find out about what happened to you?" Ruth asked her.

"After the first time that I talked to the young people, one of the kids told somebody in their family about it." She began. "And a couple of days later, Douglas told me that there's a church on the east side that wants me to come and do the same thing for them."

"That is just so awesome and I think I know who it probably was that got that goin'." Sheila said. "Do you remember the girl that I had to take out that night?"

She nodded. "Was she sittin' sort of near the back?"

"That was her and somethin' you said set her off or hit home some kind of way so you can't stop what you're doin'." Sheila said. "And you don't have to know a lot of scripture or been around forever like Aunt Frances to make a difference to people."

"Douglas told me that same thing, he said right now all I have to do is talk about what the Lord did for me and the rest of it will take care of itself." Terry said as she began to think about the experience all over again. "And I wasn't gonna tell anybody else about this but I just can't hold it." She added as she got a napkin to wipe her face.

"Don't be holdin' nothin' back, we need to hear everything because it just keeps gettin' better." Ruth told her.

"I went to the doctor for a follow up appointment yesterday and they said all of my tests came back negative, for everything." She said, lowering her voice while she openly, quietly and unashamedly cried joyful anointed tears. "No S.T.D.s, no Hiv, no pregnancy, no nothin'." She added, counting on her fingers one by one.

"Are you serious?" Sheila asked as she herself began to rejoice with her.

"They said they couldn't believe it so they did all of the tests twice." She managed to get out. "And before I left St. Louis, I had all kinds of stuff goin' on, God healed me of all of that mess that I brought on myself." She added as she quickly got up and went towards the restroom for her private moment with the God of her salvation.

"Are you okay?" A woman asked her half a minute later after she noticed her come in with tears on her face.

She nodded as she reached for the paper towel dispenser then before wetting one. "If you just knew how okay I am, you might be cryin' too." She said, shaking her head while laughing a little.

"Are you here alone, is there somebody waiting on you?" She asked out of curiosity.

"I'm here with a couple of friends and we were talkin' about it and I just lost it when I thought about what God did for me." "And I know that most people don't understand but I can't help it right now."

"Do you think your friends would mind if I sit with you because I came by myself and I would love to hear about what you're so excited about." "And my name is Kim." She added as she extended her hand.

"I mean I was one of those people that didn't care what I had to do to make a little bit of money and I didn't care who or what I had to do it with, it was my fix and I didn't know how sick I was." Terry remarked twenty minutes later as the three of them listened intently to her.

"But the Lord knew and He allowed things to happen to help you come to yourself." Sheila commented as the waiter brought their plates.

"Exactly and Sheila you don't know how sorry I am that I didn't start listenin' to Michael and Douglas when they were tellin' me what was up." Terry said.

"And everybody has a story, yours was more dramatic than most people's but God knows what every last one of us needed to get our attention."

"Are they friends of yours?" Kim asked her.

"They're my older brothers and they came and bailed me out of jail one night down in St. Louis a couple of months ago." "I got caught by a undercover cop that was bustin' hookers on the streets and me and my hardheaded self didn't get it." "I moved up here and just picked up where I left off only it wasn't on the corner but it was with anybody that would find out how easy I was." Terry said as she lowered her voice. "And I'm just keepin' it real because if I can stop just one person from makin' the same mistakes that I did it'll be worth it to me."

"It'll be more than one and I'm like Aunt Frances, you're just gettin' started.

"And I'm not braggin' about what I was but I feel this push down in me to let people know what God will do when you get to the place where you're at rock bottom and there's only one way to go and that's up."

"But you sound like somebody that's been around this for a long time and that's how we know that you're gonna do some major damage." Ruth told her.

"I mean I'm startin' to really get it now because I have all of the C.D.s of the bible classes and the Sunday services that we have." Terry began. "And when I get off from work, I have to listen to 'em over and over again until I start to understand what's goin' on and it's startin' to really click, you know what I mean?" She asked as she added sugar to her glass of iced tea.

"And it has to help to be livin' in the same house with Douglas because he knows how to really break stuff down." Sheila remarked.

"Tell me about it, I had a question about a scripture that I read one night and he was down in his office and I showed him the one that talks about love."

"First Corinthians thirteen?" Ruth asked her.

"That's the one, I remember now, and I thought I would just be in there for a few minutes because it was late." She said, remembering the night a week before.

"Not hardly, once he gets started, it's not gonna be just a few minutes." Sheila said.

"I know that now but he was explainin' to me how that if you're not lovin' people the same way that God does, anything else that you do really doesn't matter because that's the bottom line." Terry said. "And I know I was probably in there for a couple of hours because he was tellin' me about some of the stuff that him and Irene went through and other things that helped me to understand what it's all about."

"It's deep when you really get into it."

"It is but it's a good kind of a deep." Terry said as she turned to Kim who had been quietly listening to the conversation with fascination. "But what we were talkin' about before I showed up in the restroom, was when I went to the hospital yesterday for my follow up appointment after everything went down a couple of weeks ago, I found out that all of the blood tests they took on me came back negative for any kind of diseases like S.T.Ds or HIV or any of that." "And that's crazy because three months ago, we had to take some kind of work physical and I had a bunch of stuff goin' on, they gave me some prescriptions to get filled and I threw 'em away, I just didn't care." "That's how horrible I was and for God to heal me after all of that is just more than I can understand."

"But that's what the Lord does because that's what love does." Sheila said. "We might not have done all of that but it doesn't matter, the main thing is, He kept His promise when He gave us the Holy Ghost."

"And I just wish that I had known about that a long time ago because I would've saved myself from goin' through a lot of things." Terry said. "That's why I feel like I have to get to as many kids as I can because it's crazy the way they can get mixed up in stuff before they know what's happenin.'"

"Have you told Douglas that?" Ruth asked her.

"I told him that I think that I'd be able to talk to kids that are dealin' with a lot of pressure to get involved in stuff that they shouldn't be because that's how I got started when I was thirteen years old." She admitted.

"What did he think about that?"

"He doesn't have a problem with that but he said that I need to have some more knowledge about God to be able to really help people and that takes time.""And I don't have a problem with that; he said he was the same way so he understands what I'm feelin' like."

"It's like you want everybody that you know to have the same experience that you did because it's such an awesome thing." Ruth remarked.

"That's it, you said it better than I could but that's it." "I tried to tell some Facebook friends about what happened and they think I'm crazy but I don't care anymore." "All I have to do is unfriend you and that's the end of it, I don't have the time for all of that anymore."

"I hope you hold on to that kind of determination because if you do, you're gonna make a lot of difference Terry." Sheila said. "It's one thing for me to try to talk to the kids about stuff like this but I think you'll make more of an impact because you've seen so much more than I have."

"But I'm not proud of it and when I came up out of that water the night that I was baptized, I actually felt all of that stuff fall off of me; that's why I was jumpin' up and down in that pool like I was crazy but I couldn't help it." She said, laughing with them as she recalled the moment that the blood of Jesus was applied to her soul.

"That might've been the minute that you got healed, no kiddin'." Ruth said.

"I don't know when it happened, I just know that they told me at the hospital yesterday that they ran my blood tests twice because the first round just came out too clean."

"And they're just goin' by what they've seen before from other people but nothin' is impossible when you believe God for anything and everything that's a problem." Sheila said. "And that makes me think of the story that Aunt Frances told me one time that I have never forgotten."

"She is so sweet, I can't wait to talk to her again." Terry remarked.

"Are we boring you?" Ruth asked Kim then.

"Not at all, this is good stuff that I'm hearing." She said.

"We just don't want you to think we're talkin' around you so whenever you have somethin' to say, just say it, we don't bite."

"It's that I've never heard anybody talk about things like you are and it's really great to hear something positive for a change." She said after a moment as she stirred in her coke with a straw. "What happened with your aunt?" She asked Sheila, totally absorbed in the conversation.

"I was talkin' to her one night about the stuff she went through probably twenty five or thirty years ago." She began.

"Before we were born." Ruth said.

"I know, right?" "But anyway, she was tellin' me about this horrible toothache she had and she didn't even have a way to get any aspirin or anything to hold her over 'til she could get to the dentist." Sheila continued as she poured dressing on her salad. "She said all she could do was put Irene and Chris and Paul to bed because she was in so much pain, she said she told them to stay in their rooms because she had to go pray for her toothache."

"Are you serious?" Terry asked.

She nodded. "She said she was walkin' around the house holdin' her mouth and callin' on Jesus for two or three hours straight and cryin' like a baby because it was hurtin' her so much."

"That sounds like what Chris said when she was in labor for the first time." Ruth said, starting to laugh. "She said she almost felt like throwin' stuff at James."

"It must be pretty awful but anyway, she said she finally laid down on the sofa and sort of cried and prayed herself to sleep and woke up a couple of hours later and that tooth was layin' right next to her mouth where it fell out." Sheila said as she watched Terry react in shock.

"What did you say?"

"And she can probably tell it a lot better than I did but that taught me that faith is what pleases God, just like that scripture that says without it, it's impossible to please Him." Sheila continued. "How deep is that and she probably has a hundred other stories like that."

"But when you think about it, things like that shouldn't surprise us because He's God, you know what I mean?" Ruth said. "And if her faith was strong enough to even pray like that, then hey, as Douglas says, God does what He does and He does all things well."

"How do you get faith like that though?" Terry asked her.

"The same way that you got up enough faith to believe that the Lord would give you the Holy Ghost in your hospital bed like He did."

"But I didn't have any idea that that would happen, I just remember cryin' and askin' God to forgive me for all of the mess that I let myself get involved in and I needed help."

"But that's faith, somehow you figured out that He could help you plus He saw how sorry you were for all of it and that sounds like repentance to me girlfriend." Sheila told her. "And those two attitudes are what it takes for the Holy Ghost to fall, I love it."

"The only way I figured it out was because Michael and Douglas kept tellin' me things about what happened to them and then I guess I finally got it." She said.

"And that's why it makes such a difference when you talk about what the Lord has done, you just never know who you're affectin' just by sayin' a few words about what truth is."

"I tried to tell them about how much they helped me get over but it just doesn't seem like enough sometimes."

"Believe me, they know." Sheila told her.

"Girls I really hate to leave such good company but I really have to go." Kim suddenly said as she stood up. "But I would like to pay for all of your checks if that's okay with you." She said as she put a fifty dollar bill down on the table. "I just wanted to thank you for letting me sit down with you even though you don't know me."

"That's a good thing but you don't have to do that, we're okay." Sheila told her, completely taken off guard by her gesture.

"Just consider it your blessing for letting me sit down with you." She repeated as she handed Terry a business card with information on it before quickly walking away.

"I think I'm in shock." Ruth said then.

"My 2nd Chance." Terry read from the card before handing it to Sheila a moment later.

"Does it say what that is?"

"It doesn't and it sounds like a shelter or a home to me but there's no website or anything to look it up." Sheila said after turning the card over for more information.

"So what made her want to sit over here with us anyway?" Ruth asked Terry.

"When I went in the restroom, she was sittin' in one of the chairs in there and she was on her phone with somebody." Terry recalled. "And I think she thought somethin' was wrong when she saw that I had been cryin', but I had to explain to her that I was just happy and excited about what God had done for me." She said. "That's just how I said it and then she asked me if I thought you would mind her sittin' with us because she wanted to hear about it."

"Now do you see what I'm talkin' about?" Sheila asked her.

"I'm tryin' to."

"When you keep talkin' God up like you're doin', things are gonna happen." "I really don't think that it was an accident that you hooked up with her and this is gonna lead to somethin.'" She said, referring to the card that she left with them. "And I'll let you know when it happens."…

JUNE 5, FRIDAY

"I think it was Tuesday night around five or six when I was cuttin' the grass and I had no idea who this woman was." Michael remarked Friday evening at the breakfast nook with Irene and Douglas. "I looked up and there she was standin' on the sidewalk starin' at me like she was ready to jump on me with both feet." He added, referring to Barbara Mason.

"Is that when you stopped to see what she wanted?" Irene asked him.

"That's exactly what I did, I was startin' to feel like I was in some major trouble." Michael said as he broke off a slice of pizza from the box sitting on the table. "Did the kids get all they wanted?"

"Yeah they did, they're up there with Shrek and I told 'em to sit tight 'til we get ready to leave." Douglas remarked. "And it might be a minute because I need to know what went on before I go talk to her."

"She looked at me and asked me why I hadn't come by to see her like I said I would." Michael continued. "And then I thought she's got me mixed up with somebody else, I've never seen this woman before in my life."

"Did you tell her that?" Irene asked him.

"She didn't give me a chance to say anything, she just kept on yellin' so I decided to just be quiet and listen to her and that's when she started talkin' about how Phillip wouldn't like it because I had forgotten all about her." He continued. "And that's when it clicked, she thought I was Douglas and then it started to make a little sense."

"Because you've heard us talk about him huh?" Irene asked.

"Exactly and after she got through tellin' me off, she started cussin'me out and kept on walkin' down the street like nothin'." He said, shrugging a little. "And if it wasn't so sad, it might be funny but I kept rememberin' what you've told me over and over again." He said to Douglas. "There's a soul behind all of that and you can't get anywhere by bein' judgemental and lookin' the other way like they don't matter."

"It sounds like you're gettin' it and that's exactly why I'm here, I have to go over there to see what's goin' on with her." He began. "And it's been a little over three weeks since I got Sheila to go over there with me but this time is a little different."

"Do you mind stayin' with the kids for a few minutes while we go over there?" Irene asked him.

"If that's what you need for me to do, I can go up there and watch Shrek while you go take care of business with that soul." He said without hesitation. "Do what you have to do."

"I was wonderin' when you were comin', did you forget about me?" Barbara remarked ten minutes later as they walked up on her porch.

"No I didn't forget about you, don't ever think that." Douglas said. "Do you remember Irene?" He asked her as she sat down across from her.

"This is your wife isn't it?" She asked after studying her face for a moment.

"Yes ma'am it is."

"I remember you two when you got married, not long before Phillip passed."

Irene nodded before Douglas steered the conversation away from him.

"Have you been okay since the last time I was here?"

"Didn't I just see you a couple of days ago, weren't you over there cuttin' grass at your mother-in-law's house?" She asked him. "I know that I was a little rough with you but I had a date with my friend Crown Royal that night and maybe I got a little out of hand." She added, while laughing at herself.

"That was my brother, I think you got us mixed up hon." Douglas told her.

"No baby, I know what you look like." She argued. "But when I think about it, this guy that I talked to didn't have a beard like you do." She said as she suddenly remembered the difference between he and Michael.

"You're right, he doesn't.

"Phillip didn't tell me that you had a brother."

"You really haven't been able to get over that have you?" Irene asked her as she attempted to understand her grief.

"I never will and that's why I have to do things all of the time to help me forget about the night that the police came to this door and told me that my son was gone." She said with agony in her voice. "And that's why you have to come and see about me, you were the last one to see him alive so I feel connected to you because of that." She told Douglas.

"It's okay for you to feel like that but when you're lettin' that bottle make you say and do things that you wouldn't otherwise it's not helpin' anything."

"It's helpin' me to cope is what it's doin.'" She told him. "I know that you don't do that anymore and God bless you for that and I'm happy for you but until you lose a child that you brought into the world, you can't understand what that feels like." "And I don't understand how you got over it so quick, you saw it happen so how did you not lose your mind, you two were like brothers."

"I almost did and I came really close to doin' myself in because of what I saw but because there were people that had been prayin' about me and for me, the Lord kept me from takin' myself out."

"I don't think that I ever knew that about you." Barbara said, surprised.

"It's not anything that I'm proud of but whenever this comes up, I have to always tell people how powerful prayer is." "And it doesn't matter that it's been close to twenty years ago, I can't forget how close I came to leavin' here without salvation and when it comes down to it, nothin' else matters when it's all said and done."

"I go to church sometimes but that doesn't help me with bein' alone all of the time." She came back with an air of self pity in her voice.

"Do you have any family that lives here Barbara?" Irene asked her.

She shook her head. "Phillip's father died when he was about a year old so I did the best I could with him but we moved here from Houston right after we got married almost forty years ago." "I found out I was pregnant and that's what you did back in the day before everything got crazy."

"You don't have anybody in Texas?"

"I had a brother that died down there a couple of years ago but he was a lot older than me so we were never close but it just seems like death is always takin' people out of my life."

"You don't feel like you're ready to die do you?" Douglas asked her then.

"If I did, who in the crap would be here to miss me?" "If Phillip were still here, I might have grandchildren by now but since that didn't work out, what's left?" She insisted. "I get up in the mornin' and I don't have anything to look forward to so what do I have to live for?" She asked them in anticipation of an answer from them.

"I'm about to ask you somethin' and I feel like I know you well enough to get an honest answer from you." Douglas told her then.

She didn't answer but sat waiting on him to speak again.

"Was there somethin' goin' on between you and him that you're feelin' guilty about?" He asked her after a moment.

"Did he tell you about it or somethin'?" She asked him after a moment.

"No ma'am he didn't but everything seems to come back to him and that's part of the reason why I know that somethin' went down that you need to talk about."

"If he didn't tell you, how do you know?" She insisted as she began to tremble in fright.

"That's not really important right now but you need to get stuff off of your mind if you want your freedom." He told her as Irene came to her side in an attempt to calm her.

"It was a couple of days before the accident and I called and told him that I was runnin' low on money and groceries and I had a bill that needed to be paid." She recalled as she began to openly sob while still shaking. "All I needed from him was a hundred dollars and he came over here and showed me this wad of money and told me that every penny of it belonged to his drug dealer and not to bother him with my problems anymore." She managed to say.

"Keep goin', we're listenin.'" Irene urged her as she noticed Douglas' reaction to her words that triggered recollections of the life that the Lord had delivered him from.

"And that made me so upset that I told him to get out of my house and I never needed to see him again." She got out. "And two days later, he was gone, that was the last thing I said to him and I have to live with that every single day." She said, stomping one of her feet in frustration and mental pain. "That's why I have to talk to the pot in there that has his ashes in it hopin' he can hear me some kind of way." "I never got to tell him that I didn't really mean what I said."

"You've been goin' through this for almost twenty years?" Douglas asked her as he grappled with his own emotions while recognizing her need for help and compassion.

"For almost twenty years, how would you feel if that were the last thing that you said to somebody you loved?" She said as she began to raise her voice at him.

"We need to go inside with you for a few minutes." He told her as he motioned for Irene to help her stand as he started for the front door.

"Is it helpin' to talk about it after all of this time?" Irene asked Barbara as they sat down on the sofa with her a minute later.

"It helps that you're listenin' to me but it doesn't change the things that I said to him." She said after managing to calm herself.

"And you're right, you can't go back twenty years and undo that last conversation you had with Phillip." He began. "But you're makin' yourself miserable by dwellin' on it and talkin' to his ashes over here." He added with a spirit of tough love for her benefit.

She nodded a little in agreement.

"He can't hear you and as hard as it might sound to you, this is not him anyway." He said as he picked up the urn containing his remains. "This is just what was left of his body and it might help if you have this buried or scattered somewhere because it's just a reminder of the horrible thing that happened one night." He added, shaking his head as he recalled the moment in his mind.

She didn't respond but continued to listen to him.

"This won't hear or answer you but if you have any faith in God at all, that's where your help is." He told her with confidence and unrestrained belief. "When you get to the place where you find out nothin' else is workin' for you, then that's when God will prove Himself to you if you give Him the chance."

"I don't feel like I've been good enough to do that."

"How do you think I felt when I tried to ask the Lord for help?" He asked her then. "I was livin' the worst, low down, shabbiest life that you could imagine so that doesn't have anything to do with it." "Don't let the devil trick you into believin' that because that's what mercy and grace is all about."

"And if that was the case, none of us would deserve the help of God." Irene told her. "And you didn't see the shape that he was in right after this happened, it got so bad that I ended up callin' my mother because I didn't know what to do." "I was helpless."

"I didn't eat or sleep for a solid week because all I could see in my mind was this image that I'm not gonna even try to describe because you don't need to hear it." Douglas told her. "But my point is, I don't care how low or hopeless you think things are, the Holy Ghost is a comforter and it's a promise that's yours when you get to the place where you know that you need and want it." "And when I got on the phone with my mother in law that night, she said four words that basically started to change things for me because I couldn't do anything else." "She said let God help you, then she told me that she was about to pray right then and there over the telephone and I didn't have the strength to argue with her." He continued. "She started callin' the name of Jesus over me and I felt the power behind that name for the first time in my life."

"On the phone?" Barbara asked, fascinated.

"I wouldn't tell you that if it wasn't true and do you remember how much better you felt when we were here a couple of weeks ago?"

She nodded.

"Before we leave tonight, I think we need to do the same thing for you again and I'm gonna talk to my brother about a couple of things that might do you some good." He told her.

"Does that sound like a plan?" Irene asked her.

"That's the young man that I yelled at the other day?" She asked as she obviously brightened.

"He's the one." "His name is Michael and he just moved over there a couple of weeks ago and it's easier for him to check on you than it is for us because he's one street away." Douglas told her. "And we're not puttin' you off, we'll be back over here to see you but since he's so much closer than we are, it's better for both of you."

"You don't think he's upset with me do you?" She asked cautiously.

"He's not, we already talked about that with him so he knows what's goin' on with you." Douglas said as he and Irene stood up on either side of her.

"Do I get to hug you before you leave me?" Barbara asked as she slowly got up from the sofa.

"Of course you do and the next time we come, we'll bring the kids."

"How is that new baby that you brought into the world a couple of weeks ago?" She asked Douglas. "You should've seen how he handled that like he does it everyday." She said to Irene as tears began to come down her face.

"That was called doin' what you have to do, you could've done the same thing." Douglas said after a moment. "But I don't think that was just a coincidence, God knows what you need and when you need it so just look at that as the Lord lookin' out for you and He does all things well."..

JUNE 7, SUNDAY

"This is what happened and the more I thought about it, the more chills I got." Sheila remarked Sunday afternoon on the deck with Michael, Janice and Terry as they ate dinner.

"Don't leave me out, I need to hear this too." 'Nita said, overhearing her as she came out of the house with a plate. "Scoot over Michael Johnson, make me plenty of room, get as close to your sweetie as you can."

"I'm gettin' you for that later on." He told her. "C'mon, we're listenin'." He added as he urged Sheila to continue.

"You actually had to be there but Terry goes in the restroom for a minute and she comes back out of there with this woman that we've never seen before that wants to sit in the booth with us because of somethin' she said in there to her."

"She asked me if I was okay because I walked in there and I was boo hooin' like I had lost my best friend or somethin' but it wasn't like it looked."

"You and the Lord were just havin' a moment huh?" 'Nita asked her.

"You got it and I told her that I had just been talkin' about somethin' that God did for me and I lost it." Terry said. "Then she asked me if it would be okay to come and sit with us because she wanted to hear about it too."

"I thought I was crazy but even I wouldn't be that bold."

"Yeah you would 'Nita Scott, I don't believe you." Michael told her as he poured pop in his glass.

"They could've been settin' me up or somethin', people are off the chain crazy and I'm just gonna invite myself to sit down in a booth with total strangers?" "Be for real."

"And that's when Ruth started to think she might've been an angel." Sheila said, waiting on her reaction.

"She's been around Aunt Frances too much, angels don't show up in restaurants."

"Who said they don't?" "Angels can be anywhere but here's the thing." "Why would she decide to pay for all three of our checks and she didn't eat anything?"

"She what?" Michael asked.

"Before she left, she put a fifty dollar bill down on the table and gave Terry this business card." She said as she handed it to him. "What would you think?"

"I would think I was in the twilight zone or somethin.'" 'Nita said as she pulled ribs from a bone.

"My 2nd Chance." Michael read after a moment.

"What does that sound like to you?" Sheila asked him.

"Like some kind of a shelter maybe?"

"That's what I thought so I called the number that's on there to see if it was legitimate, you know what I mean?"

"So what did you find out?"

"I found out that it's a place for mothers and kids that're tryin' to get away from abusive relationships but when I asked to speak to Kim, they said they didn't have anybody there by that name."

"That's spooky Sheila, did you tell Aunt Frances about that?" Janice asked her.

"Not yet because it was just yesterday that I called this number and I asked the woman that answered the phone where this place is but she didn't want to tell me on the phone."

"Okay so what if you were one of these women that had a couple of kids and you needed somewhere to go to get away from somebody that was workin' you over?" 'Nita asked her.

"I'm gettin' to that, hold on." Sheila said. "They gave me another number to call and this one was a recording and there was a list of all these places and you had to pick from this list by the name and then it gave you the address."

"So where is it?" Michael asked her.

"I put it in my G.P.S. and it's on the east side so when we go to this church with Terry tonight, I'm gonna see if I can find it." She said as Douglas came out.

"What's the good word?" He asked as he came up behind Terry and motioned her into the house with him.

"That looked scary." 'Nita commented.

"You know Douglas is harmless, he just knows how to take care of business." Sheila said. "And I think Aunt Frances just wants to talk to her, it's all good."

"Did you get enough to eat honey?" Frances asked Terry a few minutes later as she and Douglas came in the family room where she was sitting on the sofa waiting on her.

"I probably had too much but it was hard to turn it down." She answered as she sat down next to her. "Am I in trouble or somethin'?"

"Honey don't ever think that, you're with people that love you so don't ever let those kinds of thoughts worry you."

She nodded in agreement. "Did Sheila tell you what I said?" She asked as she began to feel at ease with her.

"I missed that one, what did you say?"

"We were at dinner the other night and she was tellin' us about some of the things that you went through when Irene and Chris were kids." She began. "And I told her that I couldn't wait to talk to you again."

"And when I was down prayin' this mornin' you came to my mind and when that happens, I take it to mean that you need some kind of intercession or there's somethin' goin' on that you need help with and that's what we're here for." She said. "So I took it upon myself to take your brother aside to see what might be goin' on." She added as she glanced over at Douglas who was sitting in a nearby chair.

"The only thing that's been botherin' me is the way I keep havin' these flashbacks of what happened to me that night." She said after thinking a moment. "And every time I put all of that out of my mind, it just keeps comin' back and that's the last thing that I wanna be thinkin' about."

"Of course it is and do you know that that is an attack of your adversary the devil to discourage you and make you back up from what the Lord has done for you?" She asked her. "Satan hates the fact that you got yourself together and let God save you in such a awesome wonderful way and because He's startin' to use you to help other people by the word of your testimony, you have a fight on your hands sweetheart."

"And one of the best things about that is, the Lord gave you the power of His spirit to overcome anything that comes against you." Douglas said. "That includes people, that means thoughts that might come to your mind or whatever comes along to try to stop you in your tracks."

"I thought I was doin' somethin' wrong because all of this stuff that I used to be involved in just keeps comin' back to me." Terry said, shaking her head a little.

"And things like that are devices that the devil uses to try to lure you back out there on his territory and when that happens, you tell that spirit to get behind you in the name of Jesus and it has to obey you." Frances told her with authority in her voice. "When God gave you the Holy Ghost, that's when the war between your flesh and your spirit began and guess who the winner's gonna be when you allow God to help you?" She asked her as Douglas got up to bring Sheila, Michael, and Janice inside to hear the words of wisdom and knowledge coming from Frances.

"I love it." Terry said then as tears of joy and relief began coming down her face.

"We all have the right to love it and whatever you do, never stop askin' questions and I don't think you realize yet how blessed you are to have Douglas around to help steer you in the right direction because he's been through a lot of things."

"I'm startin' to find that out."

"And don't let anything keep you out of bible class because that's how you learn about what the Word of God tells you and that's one of your best weapons that you have against all the imps that're gonna try to throw you off."

"So is that why Irene told me there's gonna be tests that'll come up sometimes?"

"That's exactly right and if you're not stayin' as close to the Lord as you should be, things can overtake you before you know it , especially when you don't have an understanding about things." She said as Michael, Janice and Sheila came in and sat down.

"You just don't know how much better that makes me feel, I was startin' to think I had messed up somewhere."

"But even when you do make mistakes and everybody does, the Lord doesn't throw you away and leave you out there to make it by yourself." "He said that He would never leave or forsake you and this way of life has to be learned and you're not gonna get it over night."

"But I'm startin' to see what Michael was tryin' to explain to me when I first moved here and that's some of the reason that I know this is right; because of him and Douglas."

"And when you go tell about what God did for you today, you have the power to change somebody else's life like they did yours." Frances said. "You can't teach or preach to anybody yet because you're such a baby in God but sometimes your testimony can affect somebody so much that they won't be able to resist it." "When the soul hears what it's hungry for, you're gonna see somethin' wonderful, mark my words honey."

"Are you gonna be able to come?"

"I need to stay here because Chris is not feelin' good and James is with Paul and Jane helpin' them to get loaded up because they're comin' out here tomorrow." She told her. "But what I want you to do for me is to believe God with all that you have and at the same time, give the Lord praise like you never have before and watch Him do the work."

"The rest of us are goin' with you so you're not gonna be by yourself." Janice told her. "And I missed the first time but that's not happenin' again."

"And Michael she's not the only one that the Lord is gonna use because you have the chance to be a big help to Miss Barbara over there." Frances told him.

"Yes ma'am, I'm seein' that as one of the reasons why I ended up with your house." He said, agreeing with her.

"That whole thing with Donna havin' Sara right in front of her house was not an accident." She said. "And Douglas I know that wasn't an easy thing for you to do but your steps were ordered that day because that woman needs help and I'm sayin' this to all of us in here." She continued as she took Terry's hands into hers. "The Lord didn't give us the Holy Ghost to keep it hidden under a bushel because He has souls out there that need it just like we did before He saved us." "And it's too late in the day to be holdin' back when God puts people in our lives, so Douglas, I'm feelin' led to have you pray over these young kids son because we never know when somethin' may happen that's gonna put them to the test and we want more testimonies like the one this child has." She said, referring to Terry.

At that, he stood up and motioned them over to him where he proceeded to individually lay his hands and petition God for their help and strength in present and coming situations. One by one they felt the "electric" anointing of His touch through a vessel that stayed in the presence of God through constant intercessory prayer and reacted accordingly.

"Oh my God, oh my God." Terry cried after feeling the touch of God through his hands before her language suddenly changed to an unknown tongue as she willingly submitted to the God of her salvation.

"I don't know what's comin' but the Lord told me to have you do that and you see what happened." Frances said a minute later after following Douglas out into the entry hall.

"Only the Lord knows and that's all that matters." He said as he closed the french doors leading into the family room where the four of them continued to let the Lord bless them with His unforgettable presence. "But what I don't want to see is for her to get overwhelmed because this is all new to her and if we're not careful, it could go another way."

"That's the big brother in you comin' out but you know as well as I do that you were the same way." Frances told him. "And you're still that way and what she sees in you is havin' a positive influence on her." "So what you need to do is support and encourage her but at the same time, don't allow this to overtake her, just like you said."

"Believe me, I won't." He said as his phone rang. "Speak to me." He answered a moment later.

"Hey is this Mr. Johnson?" Anthony asked him after a moment.

"It is." "And who am I talkin' to?"

"This is Anthony, do you remember me from the hospital?" "I'm your sister Terry's friend."

"I remember you, what's goin' on?"

"Did she tell you that she decided not to go downtown for the lineup?"

"She did." "Is there somethin' that I need to know about?"

"I talked to one of those guys that messed her up that night and I told him about what happened to her after everything went down."

"How did you answer that?" Douglas asked him as he started out the front door.

"I told him that she's goin' to church now and that she's goin' around talkin' to kids about how she got it together and stuff." He said as he attempted to explain himself.

"Does she know that?"

"I told her that I talked to him but I didn't tell her that he wants to come and hear what she has to say so I thought I would ask you about it first."

"Did he tell you why he would want to do that?" Douglas asked him as he continued to investigate the motive of his phone call.

"That's all he said man and if you don't think that's a good idea, I'll just let him know and it won't be no big thing."

"Nobody is goin' to try to keep him out of this place but he needs to understand that it might be a good idea for him to keep a low profile." Douglas told him. "Did she tell you why she didn't go downtown for the lineup?"

"No sir." He said out of respect for him.

"She told me that it was dark in the room and she has no clue what any of those guys looked like and she didn't want to take the chance of pickin' out the wrong ones." He told him. "And F.Y.I., I'll be there for her support tonight."

"Yes sir." He said again.

"Do you mind tellin' me what his name is?"

"His name is Andre' Turner."

"I'll text you the address of where we'll be tonight so I'll see you around seven if you're plannin' to be there too."

"I told her I was comin' man because she's my friend and I just wanna hear her talk."

"When I heard about this young lady's testimony, I felt lead to ask if she could come and do the same thing here." The youth pastor spoke around seven thirty as Terry stood next to him in front of another group of teens. "This is serious business but in this day that we live in, you have a chance to be free from the spirit of this age that is causing unacceptable options like suicide and depression and I could go on and on but I'll get out of the way so that we can hear about what God has done."

"Right now I just want to thank everybody that came to listen to my experience with God." She began a moment later. "I feel like He wants me to tell you how dangerous it is to get involved in things just to be popular and accepted by other people." "That doesn't do anything but take you into places that you don't need to be and I know about that first hand." "I was thirteen years old and in the eighth grade when one of my so called friends dared me to go into the boys locker room at school and expose myself and that was the start of what made me into a sick pervert." She said as she reached for a nearby tissue. "After I got away with that, then it got around that I was somebody that would do anything and everything for the fun of it and before I knew it, I was hooked." "I lost my virginity at thirteen because of that dare I took and it got easier and easier so by the time I got out of high school, it wasn't unusual for me to be with ten or more guys in a week's time." She added as she shook her head in shame and regret as she watched the reaction of her young audience. Then instead of me growin' up, it got worse when I started to work the streets down in St. Louis when I couldn't find a job." "I figured it was quick and easy money and I had no idea that God was lookin' out for me way back then because He's like that." "He loved me enough to keep me alive in the middle of my dirt so if anybody ever tells you that you've done too much for God to help you, that is a lie." She said as she raised her voice for emphasis when she noticed a small group of five women come in the back of the small intimate sanctuary and sit down.

"Almost two months ago, that caught up with me when I got arrested by a cop that was workin' undercover down in St. Louis." She said after a moment as she collected her thoughts. "I have two brothers that live here in Des Moines and I didn't have anybody else to call to come and get me out of trouble." "I had no idea what was comin' after I made that phone call for their help, but they got on a plane, they bailed me out of jail and brought me back here because of the love of God." She purposely stressed. "They didn't judge or lecture me but they cared enough about me to tell me the truth that I had never heard in my whole life." "They told me that I have a soul that never dies and if I didn't run for my life while I had the chance, I might not see tomorrow." "God was givin' me the chance to get myself together but I thought I was too young to worry about dyin', I would think about that later on because I was havin' too much fun doin' my thing." She said in retrospect. "I wasn't walkin' the streets anymore but I knew how to find somebody that would be glad to feed the fix that I had to have." "I wasn't into drugs but it's all the same thing." "I had an addiction that I couldn't beat and one night three weeks ago, I was at a party with people that I had never met but that didn't matter to me." "I wasn't gonna pass up the chance and I didn't care that I had picked up S.T.D.s and had two abortions, it was all about me and what I wanted." She continued to her transfixed group.

"I walked up to a total stranger at this party and told him that I was available if he was interested and the next thing I knew, I was in a dark room down in the basement of this house that I had never been to in my life." "A couple of minutes later, there was two, then there were three, then four and five men usin' me up in ways that I can't even describe." "I got hit in my head, passed out and I woke up in the hospital and heard a nurse say that if I had gotten there just a couple of minutes later, I'd be in the morgue." "I had internal injuries and a concussion and these are bruises that might not ever go away." She added as she held up one of her arms. "They gave me a shot to make me sleep but nothin' they did was strong enough to get rid of the pain that I was in." "God kept me awake so I could talk to Him and ask Him for help and to tell Him how sorry I was for the way I had been livin.'" She said with an air of boldness as she wiped her face again. "I remembered what one of my brothers told me about how he gave himself up and that's when God kept His promise and gave him the gift of the Holy Ghost." "Then that's when I started to think that if He did that for him, then the same thing could happen to me because I wanted Him to forgive me and give me the strength that I just didn't have." "I was layin' there cryin' and prayin' for the first time in my life but He heard everything that I said everybody." She said in a pleading way, hoping to get her point across to them. "I didn't deserve it but He listened to me anyway and then all of a sudden I couldn't understand the words that I was sayin', I was layin' there in that hospital bed talkin' in this language that I didn't know anything about and I couldn't stop it." She said as she attempted to explain the moment that the Lord began to speak through her as evidence that His spirit had taken up residence in her mortal body.

"Then all of the pain that I was in just left." "It was gone and I was able to sit up and let God do His thing with me; He let me know that He had given me the power that I needed to live like He wanted me to." "I don't have to try to find somebody to lay around with anymore because He took all of that away." She added as she tried to contain the joy and the freedom she now had through the biblically based second birth experience.

"Those two brothers and my sister-in-law that loved me enough to tell me the truth even when I didn't wanna hear it were there at the hospital to see all of this happen to me so I have witnesses if anybody is havin' a problem believin' me." She said then. "I felt like I had left this world and when they told me that there was one more thing that I had to do, I couldn't wait to get out of that hospital to get it done." "They told me about the baptism in the name of Jesus that would wash away all of that filth and mess that I had been involved in, off of me and I couldn't wait." She repeated to her mesmerized audience that had been moved to the point of empathetic and convicted tears alike.

"They took me straight to church from the hospital and when I stepped into that water even before the man called the name of Jesus over me, I couldn't stop myself from jumpin' up and down like a kid on Christmas mornin' because I knew what was about to happen." She continued as she got a laughing response. "The blood of Jesus took away everything from the day I was born all the way to that dark room down in that basement and nobody was gonna stop me after all I had been through." She said before pausing. "And I don't know if anybody in here knows what it feels like to go to the doctor and have them tell you that they couldn't find anything wrong with you." "My blood tests came back so clean that they had to run 'em through twice and that's after I found out that I had three different S.T.D.s four or five months ago." "They didn't want to believe me when I told them that God healed me on the spot but it doesn't matter, He did it anyway." "He wants me to let somebody in here know that He can do the same thing for anybody else that believes it can happen." She said as her voice broke up when she noticed the shocked reaction of two of the women that had come in a few minutes before.

The powerful words of her testimony had "touched a nerve" and were beginning the process of transformation by faith in two more lives. Then as she stood there allowing the Lord to bless her with His undeniable presence, she happened to look up and notice Douglas and Andre' come towards her after he had asked his permission to approach her from his back seat. Then without saying a word as Douglas took the microphone from Terry and handed it to him, she suddenly remembered him as the "total stranger" that she had mentioned in her testimony.

"Do you know who I am?" He asked her then, barely able to speak.

She nodded a little as she instinctively edged closer to Douglas for support before she began to feel a sense of peace about her.

"I was drinkin' and I didn't mean for it to go like that." He said as sincere tears came down his face.

She nodded again as she was barely able to contain herself but gave herself over to the leading of her spirit that caused her to let go of any fear that would overcome her.

"I need for you to forgive me for what I did to you and I don't even know your name." He continued, his voice choking as the room went totally silent with astonishment at what was happening. "I told those guys to come into that room with me because we were about to have a good time and I am so sorry for that girl." He said with heart wrenching contrition.

"Go ahead and talk to him, let the Lord use you." Douglas quietly told her as he put his arm around her shoulder, reinforcing his support.

"I have to forgive you because God forgave me." Terry finally managed to say as she became overcome at the thought of where she could've been but for His mercy and grace. "I don't know your name either but I do know what He will do if you want Him to help you." She said as she finally made eye contact with him before he felt himself slowly shrink to the floor as he felt the presence of God for the first time.

Then as if on cue, it spread through the room like a wave, uplifting those that were spirit filled and lingering around those who had not yet tasted of His promised gift of the Holy Ghost. As Douglas helped Terry find a seat on the front row after she became overtaken by the anointed approval of her testimony, he and the youth pastor began to quietly minister to Andre' who had lost himself in his remorse.

"There's a couple of people that want to talk to you." Sheila told her ten minutes later as she sat between she and Janice.

"Are they from 2nd chance?" She asked, excited.

"That's them." "They said that they just want to meet you and give you a hug for that out of this world testimony." Sheila said as she wiped her own eyes. "And they said that they understood if you weren't up to it right now."

"Why wouldn't I be, that helps me to know that it made some difference to somebody." She said, shaking her head a little.

"I'll go tell 'em to come up here, you probably need to sit for a minute." Sheila said as she got up. "Where's Douglas?" She asked, looking around for him.

"Him and Michael went out to talk to Andre'." Janice said.

"Is that his name?" Terry asked.

Janice nodded. "Douglas knew he was comin' and he told Michael about him." "But how did that feel, do you know how powerful that was?"

"It felt a little strange because I didn't think I would ever see any of those guys but it felt good to have Douglas up there with me." She answered after a moment. "I wasn't afraid or anything but he told me to just talk to him and God did the rest."

"So how did he know that you were gonna be here?"

"The only thing that I can think of is that my coworker at the store probably hooked up with him some kind of way and told him." Terry said after a moment. "And it's probably a good thing that I didn't know because I wouldn't have been able to concentrate." She said, thinking back. "But it's all good if that made him feel any better because it helped me too.

"So what made you feel like you wanted to come in the first place?" Douglas asked as he and Michael talked with Andre' in the youth pastor's office.

"Man when I found out that she wasn't gonna come downtown to the lineup, then I started to feel really lucky like we got away with it." He said, still distressed after the short but intense conversation with Terry. "Then Anthony told me about how she was gonna come down to this church to talk about the whole thing but I didn't have no idea that it would be like that." He finished with an air of helplessness in his voice.

"What did that make you feel like?" Michael asked him.

"Are you a friend of hers?" He asked him.

"I'm her brother too but we don't want that to make you feel threatened because we're not here to come after you." Michael told him as he suddenly got up and started pacing around the room out of fear and panic.

"What are you afraid of, we're here to help you because you're havin' a hard time with this." Douglas told him as he gently took him by his arm and helped him to sit back down. "And we know about the lifestyle that she had before so nobody is judgin' you, she was the one that started the whole thing and she knows that but she got her help from God." Douglas said in an attempt to calm him down. "You heard what she said out there and the reason she was able to do that was because she knows how the Lord wiped her slate clean and started her all over again so how can she hold that against you?"

"But she could've died man, we did that to her."

"Did you hear what you just said?" Douglas asked him. "She almost left here but she didn't because the Lord spared her life and didn't allow her to." "That's why she's so willin' to go around talkin' to anybody that'll listen to what she went through, because it might help somebody else."

"I can't believe I let myself do that to her, we was usin' her like a toilet and we didn't care that she was cryin' and tellin' us to stop." He persisted as he felt the need to purge himself while sobbing like an injured child.

"Is it makin' you feel better to talk about what happened?" Douglas asked him as he began to compassionately put himself in his place, remembering his own first experience with the Lord, twenty years before.

He nodded a little, unable to talk as Douglas began to recognize the signs of a broken and contrite spirit in him which the Lord will not despise.

"Do you know that the same thing that happened to her can happen to you?" Douglas asked him as he allowed the Lord to help him be as wise as a serpent and harmless as a dove as he persistently ministered to Andre'.

As Michael intently listened and learned from the seasoned voice of a faithful altar worker, the spirit of the Lord hovered around them, ready to enter another repentant and believing heart.

"Start to thank God for His gift that He promised you if you believe it." Douglas urged him when he noticed him begin to yield himself as he suddenly threw up both of his hands upward in submission to his words.

"Give it up man, it'll be worth it." Michael told him as he recalled his experience on the day of his spiritual birthday, still fresh in his mind.

Then at that point, he began to respond to their leading, as he felt the warfare between his soul and his natural carnal mind, so unaccustomed to what was beginning to occur in him.

"I'm done, I'm done." He tearfully cried out as he looked up toward the ceiling with uplifted hands in believing anticipation of the Lord's precious promised gift of His spirit.

A few minutes later, Douglas and Michael began to lead him out of the office into the sanctuary as he fluently spoke in another tongue as God gave him the utterance, ultimate proof and evidence of the new birth experience.

As it became clear what was transpiring in front of them, all that witnessed what had happened between he and Terry, barely half an hour earlier, were totally and completely in awe of what the power of love and forgiveness had produced. She had no words to describe the joy of knowing that her testimony, coupled with the freedom that they both now possessed, had a part to play in this remarkable miracle. As she, Janice and Sheila sat there on the front row in uncontrollable tears, the sanctuary became electrified with the presence of the Lord, while Michael and Andre' circled the room together, allowing God to have His perfect way with him.

"I don't care what anybody says, there is nothing in this world that compares to this." The youth pastor spoke twenty minutes later after Andre' managed to find a seat to collapse in, drunk in the spirit of God. "This what we have seen today is what God will do when we are obedient to what His word tells us to do and young man, I don't even know your name but there's water up here just waitin' on you to come and get it."

He could do nothing except willingly nod as Michael helped him back up before he lead him to the back to prepare for his water baptism in the name of Jesus.

"And the bottom line to all of this is that Jesus is comin' back and because the scripture has told us that we don't know the day or the hour that that will happen, we have to be ready to go." "Some will go by way of the grave and the scripture says that not all will sleep but not a one us here knows if we will see tomorrow or not." He continued. "Young people are leavin' here every day of the week so if you feel the Lord dealin' with you, today is the day of salvation." He said as he motioned for Terry to come to the front again.

"I had the chance to talk to one of your brothers a few minutes ago and he informed me that it's only been three weeks since you received the Holy Ghost." He began. "And I'm here to tell you that if you continue to allow the Lord to use you like He did today, you will see Him do this over and over again."

She nodded as she willingly listened to his counsel.

"And I feel lead to ask anybody that was blessed and uplifted by the words of this testimony, to come up here so we can ask the Lord to continue to strengthen and anoint her because this could just be the beginning." "You're already ahead because you have such a wonderful example of holiness in that brother of yours with the big intimidating beard but he is obviously a humble man of God." He concluded as she became surrounded by a group of her peers that were obviously on one accord in their support of her.

As they all petitioned God as one to strengthen and fortify her for wherever she would be used to tell of His deliverance, the prayer was ended just in time to for them to witness Andre's baptism, fulfilling the scripture that speaks to born again believers:

Therefore if any man be in Christ, he is a new creature: old things are passed away; behold, all things are become new. (2 Corinthians 5:17 KJV).

End of Part 2

Printed in the United States
By Bookmasters